D1565054

On second thought… maybe I can!

A memoir by Debbie Weiss

Dear Cheryl!

It's been amazing to reconnect with you after all these years. Thank you so much for all your support!

Love,
Debbie

On second thought... maybe I can!

Copyright © Maybe I Can, LLC. 2023

All rights reserved.
No part of this book may be reproduced in any form or by
any electronic or mechanical means, including information
storge and retrieval systems, without written permission from
the author, except for the use of brief quotations in a book
review.

Cover Photo Credit: Dee Dee Designs
Author Photo Credit: Laura Billingham

ISBNs:
(Paperback) 978-1-950476-68-8
(Hardcover) 978-1-950476-69-5
(Audiobook) 978-1-950476-70-1
(eBook) 978-1-950476-71-8

Dear younger me, I want you to know that deep down, you've always had everything you need to succeed within yourself. The strength, the courage, the determination-it's all been there from the start. Even when things get tough, remember that you have an inner power that can help you overcome any challenge. Hold on tight and keep pushing forward. Know it might take some time to realize your true potential, but trust me, you've got this.

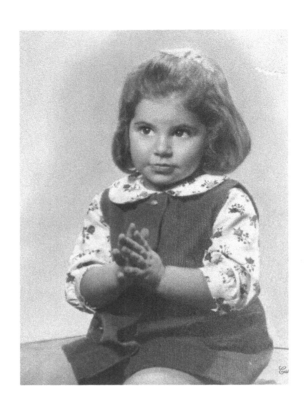

Scan the QR code to see more of my story! From the cute two-year-old above to many more moments, these pictures bring my memoir to life.

Contents

Prologue

I have been a victim for most of my life. It became my identity. Others would listen to my tales of woe and say, "poor Debbie." I was a victim of my circumstances. This was my belief until a few years ago when I came to understand that everyone could call themselves a victim if that's how they chose to live. I had no idea there was an alternative. I hadn't received the memo.

I can't pinpoint the exact moment I realized there were other options, but once I did my life was forever changed. It dawned on me that there might be others out there, just like me, who hadn't received that memo either, and I needed to make sure they did. What a wonderful and powerful realization, but there was just one problem. How the heck would I find *you* to tell my story? I could call you, but I don't have your number. I could send you an email, (which I could do if you're on my email list. If you're not, why the heck not?), but I don't have your address. I needed to figure out how to inspire people and as quickly as possible. I want you to start living the life of your dreams *now*.

So, why not write a book? Oh, I had a ton of reasons that a book was *not* the right choice.

For years, people would listen to stories about my crazy life and tell me I should write a book. I would laugh because there was not a chance in hell that I would ever write a book. My first thought was, "I can't do that. What value would my book bring to others?" After all, I don't have this amazing story of being left alone to die on Mount Kilimanjaro and lived to tell the tale, and I haven't had one big, horrible trauma (thank goodness) like others who write a memoir.

I'm just a regular person, living a regular life. I'm riding that same roller coaster as you. Sure, our peaks and valleys might not be the same, but we both have them. My first "I can't" was because I thought no one would be interested in my story. There's nothing exciting or movie-worthy about my life. BORING!

My next excuse was, let's face it, I'm not the creative type. I have an analytical mind and my careers as a certified public accountant (CPA) and insurance agent were proof of just where my strengths lie. If you're old enough to remember the book *See Dick Run*, I pictured myself only capable of writing in that simple three-word sentence format. That's only reason number two, but never fear, there's more!

My third excuse was, "I don't have the time." At this very moment in my life, I'm in a deep valley. I'm trying to run my insurance agency, while caring for my husband, Gary, who was recently diagnosed with terminal blood cancer. In addition, I have two sons who are on their way to becoming adults, but each of my family members require different levels of care.

When I'm not working or running to doctor appointments or trying to talk one of my family members off the ledge, I'm paying the bills, grocery shopping, doing laundry, and taking care of Yogi (our eleven-year-old maltipoo). *Write a book, now? Out of the question!*

My final excuse is my age. I'm too old to try something new. You know the phrase, "you can't teach an old dog new tricks"? I'm that fifty-nine-year-old dog. I prefer to think of myself as middle-aged, but *really?* It's hard to picture myself being on earth at 118 years old. I'm beginning my third and final act, and I'm too old to change. The path for the remainder of my life has already been set in stone. I'm on autopilot, so I should just sit back and try to enjoy what's left of this bumpy ride of life.

Clearly, even my excuses can't stop me since you're reading (or listening to) this book. My goal in life is to no longer give in to the "I cant's," but instead be brave enough to say, "on second thought, maybe I can!" It's a practice and a journey that I began about nine years ago, but let's start at the beginning.

On second thought... maybe I can!

Introduction

I don't know about you, but I used to hate it when editors of yearbooks would ask you to share your favorite quote. I mean, do kids that age really have a favorite quote? Maybe it's plausible by the time you graduate high school, but it wasn't for me. *Was there something wrong with my teenage self because I wasn't inspired by some random person's words?* I was born in the early sixties, so there was no Google. Heck the only computers that existed back then were huge electronic monsters that took up entire rooms. The word "Google" hadn't been invented yet.

As I got older and my photo was no longer in yearbooks. I thought I was safe, but I was wrong. My nightmare continued with the creation of social media. People would include their favorite quote in their profiles. *Really? Again, with this crap? Did people live their lives inspired by these words or was it just for show?* I wasn't going to be a phony baloney! Instead, you would always find quoteless profiles whenever you searched my name.

But then, lightning struck, and I finally became a woman with a quote. Have you ever noticed how once you stop searching in desperation for an answer or an item, it suddenly appears? Life tends to play jokes on us like that. I was sharing the story of my transformational journey, and the quote (not exactly verbatim) came tumbling out of my mouth. *Where the heck did that come from?* Whatever I said sounded good and quite inspiring—if I did say so myself. *Hmmm, had I made it up or was it an actual quote uttered by someone else?* Now that the dark ages had passed, and I had Google by my side, I quickly realized that I couldn't take credit for the words that had literally transformed my life. The credit belonged to another.

Are you sitting on the edge of your seat wondering who it was that uttered the words that changed my life? Are you guessing that it's some inspirational guru? Maya Angelou? Gandhi? Oprah? None of the above. It turns out that it's a quote I had heard over and over again from the time I was a little girl but had never paused to truly understand the meaning. As a matter of fact, it came from a movie that I had a love-hate relationship with. I hated it because so much of the movie had scenes and characters that scared me to death. It's ironic how a film that gave me nightmares contains the message that changed my life forever. Ready? Here it is:

Glinda the good witch says, "you've always had the power my dear, you just had to learn it for yourself."

POW! *Why had no one ever told me that I had the power to change and steer the direction of my life?* No teacher, professor, or parent thought that this might be useful information for me to have, apparently. I thought I didn't have any choice or control in who I was or what I did with my life. I assumed we were all victims of our individual circumstances, and our lives played out accordingly. Obviously, I knew we had some choices but not absolute power. I guess there were signs that revealed themselves along the way, but I was wearing blinders like a racehorse, only focused on the finish line.

But wait, other people seemed to have been taught this secret. *Is this something they were taught in school?* If not, maybe their parents taught them, or the more likely answer was that they possessed special qualities that enabled them to rise above us mere mortals. As I dug a little deeper, it became apparent that they were regular people just like you and me, before they became the inspirational, happy, successful people they are today.

Once the cat was out of the bag, my exciting new life journey began. I started making small changes in my daily routine. I learned that goal setting wasn't just something you did in school or at work, but you could actually apply similar techniques to *all* areas of your life. I expanded my thinking and became open to many things that I either had poo-pooed or uttered my old-favorite expression of "I can't …"

My life slowly began to change. Each day I would wake up with a renewed sense of energy and excitement. The same feeling you have when you first fall in love and each day starts with a sense of anticipation. I've got to be honest and tell you that my current everyday concerns were still there, but they didn't seem as onerous as they did before. I felt like I was finally moving my life in the direction that I wanted, one small step at a time.

I could no longer blame others or the situations I found myself in. They were not responsible for the direction of my life. With knowledge comes responsibility. I, alone, hold the power to create whatever I want in life, regardless of my circumstances. Some things are out of our control, but how we react is ALWAYS in our control. It's empowering when you realize that you have had the power all along.

"Let's start at the very beginning, a very good place to start," as Julie Andrews sang in one of my favorite movies, *The Sound of Music*. Okay, don't get nervous. I'm not going to give you a year-by-year synopsis of my life story. After all, my goal is to inspire you, not put you to sleep. This book will share with you who I was, who I was becoming, and who I am still becoming. In sharing this, my goal is to inspire you to dig deep and do some soul searching of your own. Doing so will help you identify the barriers that might be stopping you from living life on your own terms. My stories will highlight why and how I perceived myself and the world around me.

You see, we all have a set of core beliefs, which are formed by the age of seven. These beliefs are lurking in our subconscious minds and are partially responsible for how we think today. These are assumptions or perceptions that we have about ourselves that help to form our identity. They are often negative, inaccurate, and hold you back from achieving your potential. They could come from your peers, teachers, parents, or others you encounter. Your experiences, education, and family beliefs can also play a part in forming these assumptions. Pretty much anything and everything that has ever happened to you in your life contributes to those core values and thoughts.

It doesn't mean that everyone set out to cause you harm with what they said or did. Chances are, those who caused you to internalize these negative opinions about yourself had no idea what their actions or comments were doing to you. It's ironic because the more I explore my own limiting beliefs from my past, my mind turns to my own children. *Oh no! What have I said or done to screw them up?* It kept me up many nights, playing each moment of their lives out in my mind, trying to see where I went wrong, until it hit me. I did the best I could at the time. I would never, ever, do anything to maliciously harm my child's psyche in any way. It upsets me to think that I probably have contributed to their own negative opinions in some way.

I have to remind myself that I'm not perfect. None of us are. Chances are there is no one in this world who doesn't grow up with at least a few negative views of themselves. The good news is that once we are aware of what they are and where they came from (which does take some time and energy to figure out), we can begin the process of removing them and replacing them with positive, accurate thoughts. Our brains are quite magnificent, highly efficient, hard drives that can be rewired.

Once I became aware of this concept, it was apparent to me that many of my limiting beliefs were tied to feelings of shame, insecurity, and fearfulness, which were formed during childhood. However, I had never given much thought to some of the other ideas that might be lodged deep in the caverns of my subconscious. This journey into the deep end is going to take a bit longer and is still ongoing.

For as long as I can remember, my lifelong mantra has been "Why me? Why does everything bad happen to me?" I was always throwing the best and biggest pity party with lots of cookies and ice cream.

Understanding that others also have thoughts and emotions that are guiding their decisions without them even being aware, helped the pity parties come to an end. There is not a human on the face of this earth who doesn't have trauma. I never realized that trauma could come in different shapes and sizes. To me, a traumatic event is one that most people would recognize, such as a plane crash or the sudden, unexpected loss of a loved one. However, there are also little traumas in life that we all experience.

The other truth that took me fifty years or so to uncover is that just because I think it doesn't mean that it's true. Who knows why that truth never dawned on me. I wasn't consciously saying to myself, "I thought it, so it must be true." Nope. I was subconsciously assuming that my thoughts were hard truths. The sense of freedom I discovered when realizing this wasn't reality, if I didn't want it to be, was empowering. This meant that all those negative thoughts I had about myself were not necessarily true—all these years I had been lying to myself.

So, if I've been telling myself lies all along, I now have the ability to tell myself the truth. The hard part is recognizing when I'm having an unhelpful or untruthful thought and then letting it fly right out of my head, so I can replace it with a helpful one. I make it sound like a piece of cake, but it's not, it's a daily practice. However, over time it does get easier and becomes second nature.

By sharing my stories, my goal is to inspire you to step into your *own* power. Even if you haven't tapped into it recently, that power is still inside you. It makes no difference if you are young or old, rich or poor, experiencing trauma or not. There is no valid reason for you to not take control of your life and steer it in the direction of your dreams. It won't happen overnight. It's a lifelong practice, but today is the day that practice begins.

Let's get started!

On second thought... maybe I can!

Part I

Discovering: The Past

♥ 1 ♥
In the Beginning

"When you're different, sometimes you don't see the millions of people who accept you for what you are. All you notice is the person who doesn't." –Jodi Picoult

Ever since I can remember—as well as prior to that (I'm guessing since birth, even though I can't say I recall)—my life's theme has been my weight. Now, hold on and don't roll your eyes at me. Even if weight hasn't been your life's theme, the emotions I dealt with and the lessons I learned are universal no matter what you struggle with.

Maybe you weren't a good student growing up and were made fun of or made to feel dumb. If so, I hope you know that you are NOT dumb at all! I know for a fact that you are quite intelligent. After all, you're clearly very smart based on the books that you read. (Wink! Wink!) The point is that you can substitute any word for weight and be able to see yourself in my story.

My negative beliefs about my weight began on October 9, 1963 (the day I was born), or that's how I see it because my parents would always remind me how I was born at 11:40 a.m., right in time for lunch! Or how the pediatrician told my mother

15

to switch me from regular milk to skim milk when I was six months old because I was gaining weight too quickly. These little "jokes" were told over and over and over again to anyone and everyone who would listen. *Ha Ha!* I would pretend to find it amusing, chuckling with the audience.

Your weight is something that you literally carry with you wherever you go, for all to see. Keep in mind that back in 1963 the world was a very different place than it is today. Body positivity was not a thing. Instead, there was Twiggy. Now if you're not from my generation and have no idea what or who I'm talking about, Twiggy was a supermodel in the 60's and 70's, and her body type was that of a twig. Literally, a skinny twig with absolutely no meat on it. She was the ideal body type. No curves, rolls, or cellulite allowed. She was who women aspired to look like regardless of their own natural body type. I was definitely born in the wrong decade, unlike my mom.

My weight seemed to rear its ugly head in all aspects of my life. We are literally tied together at the hip (large hips they are). You see, my defense mechanism, trying to poke fun at myself before someone else does, is still there. My stories will illustrate how my weight and the way that others treated me has defined my life. I'd like to say this is no longer the case, but I'd be lying. As I said earlier, I'm a work in progress.

♥ 2 ♥

Dance Class

"No one can make you feel inferior without your consent."
—Eleanor Roosevelt

Let's face it, good, bad, or indifferent, our parents are typically our first role models. They are human, so they have both desirable and undesirable traits—just like us. Of course, we don't usually realize they don't walk on water until something happens, and we become disillusioned when we learn they're just mere mortals. It's an awful realization, similar to when you learn the truth about Santa. You just wish you could rewind the clock a minute or two before the discovery. I idolized my parents and wanted to be just like them.

My parents met at Camp Chicopee in Galilee, Pennsylvania when they were kids. Back then, it was fairly common for East Coast Jews to attend sleep away camp in the mountains every summer. Picture the set of *Dirty Dancing* but with kids and bunks and ballfields. Their parents would drop them off and would visit a few times a summer to spend the weekend.

My dad was seven years older than my mom, so he was a counselor, and she was a camper when they met. My dad was handsome, funny, athletic, charming, and a natural performer. He loved to be on stage and was a pretty good singer and dancer. He was considered a "catch" by his fellow campers and counselors.

My mom was athletic, thin, attractive, and a good dancer and singer too. They enjoyed and excelled at many of the same things. They married when my mom was nineteen years old (which seems crazy young now!), and they were touted as the king and queen of Camp Chicopee. I entered the scene two years later, and then my brother Michael rounded out our family when I was four years old.

My parents' love for music rubbed off on Michael and me. Whenever we took car rides, we would turn on the radio and sing songs together at the top of our lungs. Unfortunately, I inherited their love for music and not their singing voices. I was pretty tone deaf and could never sing as beautifully as they both could. At home, I would be completely entranced when they would put a record on the stereo and dance the Lindy. They looked so effortless and in sync with each other as they glided across our living room floor. Oh, how I longed to be in the arms of a man just like my dad who would lead me gracefully around the dance floor. My natural affinity towards dance was luckily better than my singing, and I couldn't wait to start learning how to dance just like they did.

In the 70s kids didn't participate in activities in a formal setting until they were in kindergarten. I was counting down the days until I could enroll in dance class. Ballet didn't thrill me, but those tap shoes were something I longed to put on my feet. When the time finally came, my excitement bubbled out of me like a soda bottle that was shaken up before unscrewing the cap. It just couldn't be contained. My mom and I went shopping for all the things that were needed, including ballet slippers, tap shoes, a body suit (pink of course), tights (also pink), and a pink tutu to complete the outfit.

My mom warned me not to rip anything or get it dirty when we got home, and I rushed to tear open all the packages to try everything on. I then proceeded to prance around the house, but not in tap shoes because they could ruin the floor (that's what Mom told me), swirling and twirling in delight. I rushed downstairs to the front door the minute I heard my dad's key turn and click the lock open. He told me how great I looked and applauded my spins and leaps.

The day of my first dance class, I couldn't focus during the school day, which was pretty unusual for me since I loved school and learning. That day I was trying to calculate how much time remained between being stuck in my kindergarten classroom and going to dance class. When the moment the bell rang, I raced home, alternating between a skip and a run, ripped off my school clothes, and dragged on those tights (I understood why they called them tights, yikes!) and bodysuit. My mom needed to help a little because getting those tights up and over my chubby legs, without putting a hole in them, was no small feat. I was dressed and ready to go early, so I sat down to watch *Bewitched* on our kitchen television, waiting for Mom to give me the signal that it was go time.

I took one step through the dance studio doorway, and my overwhelming excitement turned into impending doom when I saw all the other little girls dressed in their leotards and tights—some pink, some white, and some black. They looked different from me. Their dance costumes fit them a lot better. None of them had a little roll that protruded from their bodysuit, above the line where the tights clung to their stomachs. I saw no other legs that looked like mine. Everyone else's legs were thin and smooth, not lumpy and bumpy.

Alert! Change of plans! I was outta there. I turned around with my coat still on and grabbed the handle of the door. Just as I was about to turn the knob, my mother's hands covered mine and informed me that we were not leaving. I had no choice but to take my coat off and expose myself to these mini-Twiggy's. I cried and complained and the only way I was coaxed through those doors onto the shiny floors of the studio was because they let my mom come in there with me. I was furious with her. *Didn't she love me? How could she not protect me from this uncomfortable situation where I clearly did not belong?* I really hated her at that moment. For not seeing how scared I was and for stopping me from escaping out into the asphalt parking lot into the safety of our teal, 1968 Chevrolet Impala.

My cheeks turned a rosy color as all the girls were chatting while looking around and checking each other out. The teacher moved to the front of the room, gave us some instructions and, being the good student that I was, I memorized all that she said. She walked to the corner of the room to put the record on, so we could dance. As the music filled the room, my body took over. Thoughts of my lumps, bumps, and rolls fled from my mind like a boy who had just stolen a piece of candy from Woolworth's (it was a big thing back then, both stealing candy and Woolworth's).

As the record started making a scratching sound to signal it had ended, something had changed. Everyone was looking at me but for very different reasons. They were shocked to see the little, chubby girl could move and remember the steps so well. My chest began to swell with pride, and I stood up a little taller.

The only area of my life where I was consistently praised was as a student. I certainly did my homework and studied for tests, but the fact was that it came very easily to me. I wasn't one who put in a lot of effort or time but was lucky enough to still be successful. It became my identity. Debbie was smart even though she was chubby. Anything related to my body tended to end in disaster, so to receive attention for my dancing was something I had never experienced.

Let's go! I was ready to dance. Now, I wanted to have everyone's eyes on me. I craved to hear their words of praise and to be seen not as a chubby girl but as a good dancer. I had to be patient and wait several minutes because most of the girls in the class were not as adept as I was (if I do say so myself). The teacher had to slowly break down the steps over and over again until she finally picked up the record needle and gently placed it back down on the record, so we could dance again.

After class ended, the teacher came up to my mother and me and said I was a natural. It was official, dance class became my obsession and my passion. During the week, I would put on my pink tights and bodysuit and practice my steps while counting down the days until our next class. Week after week this pattern continued, through to spring when the teacher announced that it was time to get ready for the recital.

A recital sounded scary and exciting all at the same time. I was going to be on a stage, dancing in front of an audience. We would perform one dance, which was a bit disappointing. I mean, if I was going to have my moment on stage, I wanted to stay out there for as long as possible. Then, the teacher opened her mouth and spoke the words that would change my life forever, "Debbie, you will be the lead dancer."

Containing my excitement was nearly impossible. It was as if I won the lottery, and I wasn't allowed to scream. It was painful, but I knew it was bad manners to gloat. Naturally, after class, I was able to let the cork pop and explode. I called all my relatives to share the news. I fell asleep with a smile on my face that was still there when the morning sun peeked through the curtains in my pink bedroom.

I couldn't wait to begin learning and practicing my leading role. The following week, I ran through the doors into the dance studio and was a few minutes early. I saw the teacher and one of the moms talking and looking at different colored costumes. I wondered which one would be for me. I guess back then the studio had the same costumes they re-used from year to year. You didn't have to make or buy your own.

Right on cue, they called me over. They needed to see the "star" (they didn't say that that's just what I was thinking). The mom started to bend down and then held up a measuring tape. As soon as I saw that white and black monster, dread started to form and rise from my toes to my fingers. She started circling the monster around different parts of my body, then declared for all to hear, "the costume won't fit her, it's too small."

I ran out of the room crying, and I never went back.

My parents tried to persuade me to return, but I wouldn't budge. I had been completely humiliated and it was clear that a fat girl like me did not belong in a tutu. At school I would run to the bathroom crying when my friends were excitedly talking about dance class and the upcoming recital. Every day was torture and reminded me just how much I didn't belong. I was unable to do what I had always wanted to do. The only dancing I could do was in my bedroom, all alone.

My life was cursed—cursed by this extra weight that I carried. I didn't understand why my body looked like it did. I just wanted to look like everyone else. *Why was I so unlucky?*

On second thought… maybe I can!

♥ 3 ♥
Torture at school

"Always remember you are braver than you believe, stronger than you seem, and smarter than you think." –Christopher Robin

How old are you in first grade? Six or seven, I think. At such a young age, I was already ashamed of how I looked, scared of just about everything and everyone. In my mind, I was convinced that everyone was judging me. I can't imagine that there is anyone on this planet who hasn't been negatively impacted in some way from an experience they had in elementary school. We all have stories where we felt shame or embarrassment in front of our peers. Decades later, the scars remain. For me, my insecurities around my weight added fuel to the fire. Recalling them now, still vividly brings back the emotions I felt back then.

I began looking at the clock about fifteen minutes before the bell would ring for lunch at 11:45 a.m. I was in Miss Logus' first grade class, sitting in the second row from the door, fourth seat in the row. When you have a last name that begins with the letter "S," you get used to that seat placement since we always sat or lined up in alphabetical order.

I started to feel like I really needed to pee and was wondering if I could make it another fifteen minutes. My eyes were transfixed on the big black hand on the clock hung right above the door. The door where I needed to make my exit and run down the hall to the left, into one of the three stalls in the girl's bathroom at Plaza Elementary School in Baldwin, NY (on Long Island). It seemed like the clock was broken or out of batteries because nothing seemed to be happening as I stared at the hands, willing them to tick faster.

At 11:37 a.m., I realized I wasn't going to make it, so I raised my hand to ask if I could go to the bathroom, but Miss Logus wasn't looking in my direction. She seemed to be glancing everywhere except at the back corner of the room, where I sat, bouncing my legs. I could feel the panic begin to rise through my body. With my hand still meekly raised, I considered my options.

Option 1: I could call out while she was talking and say, "excuse me Miss Logus, may I go to the girl's room?" The problem with this was that everyone would turn around and stare at me. In other words, I would've rather shriveled up and died right there in that seat. If I didn't shrivel then I might get in trouble for calling out during class. Forget that option.

Option 2: I could just get up and start walking to the door and when the teacher sees me, I can explain that it's an emergency. Strike two—not a chance because then all twenty-eight pairs of eyes would be focused on me and every move I made. That was even worse than option 1.

Option 3: I could concentrate on something else besides this increasing urge to pee and hold it until the bell rings, at which point I could dash out the door weaving in and out of the swarm of hungry grade schoolers, rushing to the cafeteria. This seemed like the only viable option.

I did not choose wisely. Turns out that my six-year-old brain was not developed enough to concentrate on something else and prolong the inevitable. Can you guess what happened? Yep. You guessed it! I peed right there in my seat just a minute or two before the bell rang. Just in time for those around me to see the puddle that was under my desk and chair, as well as the fresh pond that was forming on top of my desk as the tears flowed down my face. At that moment, I wanted the ground to open and swallow me up, so I wouldn't have to deal with the shame and embarrassment of the situation.

As the other kids filed out of the room, Miss Logus took my hand, gave me a tissue, and led me out of the classroom. We walked down the hall to the nurse's office where they happened to keep a stash of clean underwear, which I squeezed into, since most girls my age wore a smaller size. The nurse called my mom and asked her to come pick me up because I was distraught and unable to finish the day.

Seeing my mother walk through the door of the nurse's office caused a new flow of tears to arise. I ran to my mother, my safety net, and squeezed her as tightly as I could thinking that I wanted to just stay with her, so I would be safe. Protected from the terror of humiliation.

My life seemed on track to be quite an agonizing journey. I couldn't seem to escape the pain of being humiliated. Back in the late 1960's and 1970's, kids had to wear gym suits to participate in gym class—at least this is how it worked at my school. Every year my mom and I would make the annual, dreaded trip to the local army/navy store (I have no idea why they were sold there) and try on the sack of horrors. It was a yellow "dress" with snaps up the front with a matching yellow fabric belt that cinched at the waist. The dreaded cinch would cause, at least in my case, the pleated skirt bottom to stick out and accentuate my large hips while simultaneously exposing my tremendous thighs.

This torture suit never fit me correctly, so I would have to buy a larger size to fit over my hips and then would have to have the length taken up (not that I wanted to expose my legs, but it was better than the alternative), so it wasn't hanging down past my knees. Of course, just to add to the horror of it all, it came with matching bloomers. I needed to buy an even larger size suit to get the bloomers large enough to fit. Even the ones that "fit" had elastic edges that would dig into my skin and pinch me. I couldn't see how anything could possibly be worse.

I never wanted to change in the locker room at school because I didn't want the other girls to see me in my underwear. So on gym days, I would wear the yellow monstrosity to school in the morning, with pants over the bloomers—what a sight that was! Not to mention how uncomfortable it was to be wearing yellow puffy bloomers over my underwear topped off with my pants over them both. It was clear the entire world was against me.

So, I would go to gym class, in that golden dress, and the mean gym teacher with the raspy voice would line us up and turn on a recording that walked us through our warmup. The title was called, "Chicken Fat." I silently prayed each time I stepped into that gym that the record had gotten scratched, and a replacement could not be found.

If you've never heard of this little ditty, it's a song that leads you through a series of exercises, like toe touches, push-ups, trunk twists, and running. Part of the chorus was "go, you chicken fat, go away". This line was sung over and over again. The last part of the song, which tells you to "run like a tortoise, too far and too slow." It then made you speed up like a hare, and at the end, everyone was supposed to tell that "chicken fat to go away." You might imagine how being the fattest, or at least one of the fattest kids in the class, would make it tough to get through even one chorus of this song, let alone multiple, without being stared at and teased. The gym suit situation just added to everyone else's enjoyment, and my complete and utter embarrassment.

It's quite a coincidence that I was often feeling feverish or had a stomachache on the days I had gym. I was okay when we were playing volleyball or square dancing, but the stomach aches grew more and more frequent during the gymnastics unit and the most dreaded Presidential Fitness Tests. Every year, every student was required to participate in a test that consisted of six sadistic activities: curl-ups, pull-ups, push-ups, the sit-and-reach, the thirty-foot "shuttle run," and the one-mile endurance run. I didn't need to fake a stomachache when we were forced to participate, I truly was sick to my stomach.

Naturally, we would all be watching each other, and everyone was bragging and boasting about how many pull-ups they did or how little time it took them to complete the mile run. I scored a zero in all the "ups." Of course, I could do a curl-up, the equivalent of a modern-day crunch, except for the fact that you had another kid holding your feet down and deciding whether you were using proper form, thus being worthy of being counted. If I was lucky enough to get another poor chubby or unathletic girl as my partner, the number I completed correctly improved. However, there was never an improvement with the pull-up and push-up. I couldn't even hang from the bar, let alone pull myself up, so there was no possibility of faking it.

Then there was the running. In my case, it was never really what you would call "running," it was more like a slow jog. We would all run the mile together, starting at the line when the "gun" went off, just like we were Olympians. As in any race, there were pace setters, sprinters, the middle of the pack, and then there were the few slow pokes bringing up the rear. I wasn't bringing up the rear, I *was* the rear! As a matter of fact, after a quarter mile, my slow jog turned to a walk because I was panting, trying to get some air into my lungs. There was everyone else at the finish line, watching, pointing, and laughing as I strolled across the line, dead last.

In those days, everything was a competition. In addition to the Presidential Fitness Test, each year we would have to run the 100-yard dash. I guess there wasn't enough room in the gym, and there was no track at our elementary school, so we sprinted in the dead-end street where the school was located. There would be two gym teachers with stop watches and two lines, so everyone was paired up to run against one another. They would set up those orange and white cones at the start and finish line, and everyone would watch and cheer (or jeer) as the races were run.

In the week leading up to the race, I would have nightmares where I'm once again paired up with a child who looks like a gazelle, and all eyes are on me because they can't wait to see just how slow I am. I would wake up in a dripping sweat, scared out of my mind that my nightmare would become a reality.

It's such a coincidence (Wink! Wink!) that I would seem to come down with a deadly plague every year just prior to this event. Unfortunately, I still would have to run it, but it typically wouldn't be in front of the rest of the class, just in front of the other poor souls who also happened to be "sick" that day too. The dread and embarrassment that I felt was not just from the other kids, but also from my gym teacher. It was something about her tone and the way she looked at me that I felt the disgust dripping from her eyes when she watched me.

Naturally, at our elementary school, she was the girls' gym teacher every year. There was never hope for a reprieve. I knew the torture would continue year after year. Our elementary school was K-six, and then we moved onto junior high school. So, in sixth grade you were the "big kids on campus." I was excited that this would be my last year with Ms. Raspy Voice, but I was shocked to learn on the first day of sixth grade that she had retired, and we would have a new gym teacher named Ms. Henskin.

Now, this could've been a good thing or a bad thing—better to dance with the devil you knew. Ms. Raspy Voice already knew that I couldn't run like a "hare" in the "Chicken

Fat" song or pull myself up (or even hang) from a bar. *But what if this new lady was even tougher? What if she found new ways to torture and embarrass me?*

At first glance, she appeared to be nice, but I was leery. She was much younger than Ms. Raspy Voice, and she had a blond pixie haircut with a normal voice. Ms. Raspy Voice had short gray hair and a very husky, gravely, distinctive voice. This woman actually seemed pleasant, and she seemed to have never heard of the "Chicken Fat" song. These were all very promising signs.

As the year began, something quite unusual happened. Ms. Henskin liked me and saw potential in me. She recognized that I might not be fast or have upper body strength, but I was coordinated and athletic. She praised me for my ability and actually chose me to be in three out of four after school sports teams (not soccer since that involved a lot of running). Many of the girls who had made fun of me for years began to treat me a bit differently, as I was now their teammate, their equal who contributed to the team. By this time, I had also learned that I was better off poking fun at myself and making fat jokes before anyone else could. I was "affectionately" called "big mama" and "thunder thighs." Outwardly, I took them as terms of endearment, even though it hurt so much on the inside.

But I began to enjoy gym class and became a leader. Ms. Henskin had single-handedly changed my life and there was a small drop of confidence now running through my insecure veins. I don't know if she realized how much she was helping me, but I'm hoping she did. What a difference someone can make when they respect and accept you. She saw that I could still be an athlete, regardless of my weaknesses. For the first time, I began to truly believe that I was athletic, despite the extra weight I carried. Thanks to Ms. Henskin, gym became one of my favorite classes.

On second thought… maybe I can!

♥ 4 ♥
Am I in the Right Family?

"To be yourself in a world that is constantly trying to make you something else, is the greatest accomplishment."
—Ralph Waldo Emerson

I think I was born into the wrong family. I was a fat girl living with a bunch of skinny people who couldn't relate to my experiences living in a chubby body. My mom was my role model, but I wasn't anything like her. In fact, I was just the opposite. She was thin, pretty, athletic, and confident. She never seemed afraid of anything, and there was nothing she couldn't do. She was very smart, and even though I knew I was smart, I was way out of her league. I would constantly compare myself to her. I knew I was lacking most of her positive traits, so I never felt good enough. *What's wrong with me?* I thought.

My brother who is four years younger than me was a string bean too. Maybe somehow, they mixed the babies up in the hospital, and I was really the daughter of a fat family. A fat family like my cousins were lucky enough to live in. My aunt and uncle were heavy and so were their three daughters, who were all around my age. Unfortunately, we didn't get to see them much because we were in Long Island, and they were in

New Jersey. My cousins had a mom who got it. My aunt knew what it felt like to not be able to wear the same clothes as her friends. She knew where to shop, so the girls weren't wearing something that made them look like they were old ladies. There were hardly any clothing options near me if you didn't fall into the "regular" sizes. Often, we would have to visit the boys' husky department to find jeans that fit me.

In Long Island, there was only one store where I could shop called "Trim Town." What a name! I hated going there because every single time my mother and I would have an argument. I would put the clothes on, and she would always have to fix how they were laying on my body because I didn't know how to put them on correctly. I would hate every piece of clothing I tried on because it was demoralizing to look in the mirror and see the reflection of a body that I abhorred. At the same time, I'd see my mother who was a size six, staring and critiquing my outfit.

According to my cousins, they had lots of stores in New Jersey that catered to chubby girls. My cousins never complained about being teased either. It seemed to me that life for a fat girl was much better over the border in Jersey. Maybe there, no one noticed body size. Clearly, my life would be so much better if I lived there. They were so lucky to have fat, loving parents who completely understood all the challenges of being overweight.

Okay, I don't want to make it seem like my mother was constantly mean to me because that wasn't the case. She just couldn't relate and saw how miserable I was with my body, so she would try to help. One of the ways she "helped" was limiting my food intake. She would put me on these diets and hide food around the house, so I wouldn't know it was there and wouldn't be tempted. I was allowed to have two pieces of melba toast with one piece of "diet" American cheese for breakfast. YUM! Oh, how I despised that melba toast. The only good thing about it was you couldn't eat it too quickly because it was so hard that it would cut the inside of your mouth when you bit into it—it was best to take your time.

I soon learned where all the food hiding places in the house were. I mean, after all, how is someone supposed to be happy living on melba toast? The rest of my meal plan followed suit. The portion size was next to nothing, and the food was bland or outright disgusting. Mom put me on a diet that was less than 1,000 calories per day, which was the norm for diets in the seventies.

The wok, breadbox, or oven always had tasty treats that I would sample when no one was around. Each time I found a hidden item, it felt like I had hit the jackpot. I would tell myself that I would only eat a small amount because if I ate a lot of it there would be an interrogation after the fact when someone discovered some had been eaten. Guess what? Who could eat just one or two Oreos? Not me. The next thing I knew, instead of eating a couple, there were only one or two Oreos left in the box. *Crap! I did it again*, I would think to myself. It was just more proof that I was a bad person who couldn't control herself around food.

At the age of ten, my mom realized that I needed someone else to supervise me, since I was having no luck with the diets she had put me on. So, she came with me to attend my very first Weight Watchers meeting. Weight Watchers was only about ten years old at the time, the same age as me. The diet was very strict and limiting. I didn't like any of the food choices that were on their plan, but I had to try it because I was desperate to find the answer to my problem.

I became a Weight Watchers dropout after only a few weeks. The program was too rigid, especially for a young, picky eater like me. It seemed the only thing you were allowed to eat was lettuce and tuna fish. I hated tuna fish, so eating like a rabbit could only last for so long. Don't get me wrong, I wanted to lose weight. It's not like I felt good in my skin. I was absolutely miserable and wanted to continue the search for a solution. I would daydream about finding some magic program where I would lose weight and still be able to eat what I wanted. Unfortunately, that program didn't exist.

After I failed at Weight Watchers, we moved on to my pediatrician. He was a nice man with a pot belly who was always kind when discussing my weight. He wasn't the type of doctor who berated you for being overweight like so many others. He gave me a fairly manageable food plan, and I would walk to his office after school every Monday and get weighed. It was the spring and summer prior to Junior High School (which back then meant seventh grade), and I was doing pretty well. I lost a good amount of weight for the first time in my life. I was feeling good about myself—until the usual thing happened. By October, I had regained all I had lost, plus a few pounds more. *"What the heck is wrong with me?"* I asked myself. *"Why am I such a pig?"*

The same loop would play over and over again in my mind. I was miserable about my weight, and my mom watched everything that went into my mouth like a hawk. If I went into the kitchen to grab a snack, there was always a look to see what I had taken followed by a comment. Food was still being hidden, but the hiding spots would change when I discovered the hidden treasure.

There was one instance when I was unaware there was cake hidden in the house. Evidently, my brother wanted a piece, and I was upstairs, so my mother cut him a slice and told him to go into the other room, so I wouldn't see him. I came down a few minutes later, walked into the room where my brother was scoffing down a big piece of chocolate cake. I yelled, "where did you get that?" He apologized and told me Mom gave it to him, and that he was hiding, so I wouldn't see.

You would think that since food was constantly being withheld that I would have been able to lose weight and maintain the loss, but that was never the case. I wouldn't only binge on the forbidden food hidden around my house but also eat delicious snacks at my friends' houses, school, birthday parties, and holidays. At home, I was permitted to eat whatever the family was having for dinner, unless I was on a diet. I was able to get reprieves in between failures.

The clothing situation only grew more difficult as I reached adolescence and couldn't wear the cute outfits my friends wore. My aunt would come to the rescue and bring me to New Jersey for a weekend of shopping, eating, and hanging out with my cousins. I was so comfortable there that a part of me wished I could live with them, even though I knew I would miss my family—even if they were skinny. So, I would return home to try and figure out how to survive as the fat girl in a skinny family once again.

♥ 5 ♥

The Dreaded Belt

"Children are like wet cement. Whatever falls on them makes an impression." –Dr. Haim Ginott

For most of the twentieth century, spanking and whooping your child was a fairly common discipline. My grandfather had disciplined my father and aunt this way, so my father applied the same tactics on my brother and me. Each time I was spanked, it was traumatic. It continually confirmed my belief that I was unworthy—although the spankings were not tied to my weight.

The problem was my mouth. Yeah, yeah, I talk a lot, but that wasn't the issue. It was that tone of mine. I'm not very good at hiding my feelings or opinions. I don't wear my heart on my sleeve, it's actually on my face and too often comes out of my mouth. Countless times I've been told, "it's not what you say, but how you say it."

Most of the time that tone was directed towards my mother. Hearing my father say, "don't talk back to your mother" should have been the warning sign for me to shut my mouth and get my turned-up nose back into its regular position. But no, I just couldn't let it go. The anger I was feeling didn't allow me to stop talking. I had to get it out, and the only way I knew how was with my words ... and my tone.

Without pausing to reflect, another snide comment would inevitably come tumbling out, causing steam to come out of my father's ears. His face would turn red, and simultaneously, he would begin to scream and reach for his belt. He was a pro, just like a cowboy drawing a gun. He could unbuckle that belt and pull it out of the loops of his pants in one swift motion. Our dog, Chuckles, would tremble in fear and escape to hide under the dining room table. Poor little thing didn't know it was me who was in for it and not him.

I would start to run, trying to get upstairs to hide under the bed the minute I got a glimpse of that steam. There were a few problems with this plan, however. The first was that I was slow, and my dad wasn't. He would skip steps, so he only needed to go up eight to my sixteen. The second was that I was always cornered. I quickly learned that locking my bedroom door was not smart. If I miraculously beat him to my room, slammed the door, and clicked the lock, it would only make things worse. It would kick his rage up another notch, so when he eventually got in my room, I was in for an even more painful experience.

Going under the bed seemed like a good idea. After all, he was a lot taller and bigger than me, so he couldn't get me. However, it was difficult for me to shove my chubby body all the way underneath the bed frame. I would try to shimmy my way underneath with the wall as my finish line. It was a similar motion to me trying to get a pair of tight jeans over my thighs and hips. One of two things would happen. He would either get to me before I had time to work my way underneath, giving him the opportunity to grab one of my extremities that hadn't yet made it to safety, or he would come in and just move the bed.

Duh!

Common sense did not seem to come naturally for me, and this is a perfect example. At this point, I would sense defeat and shift my focus on figuring out how to protect myself from the pain and torture that was about to ensue.

With his face red as an apple, he would tell me how this hurts him more than it hurts me. He would then pull down my stretch pants and firmly push my stomach onto his knee, leaving my backside exposed. Now seriously? Did he expect me to believe that *this* was more painful for him?

At this point I would be begging, "daddy, please don't hit me. I'm sorry, I'll never do it again." My apology would come too late. As his hand lifted the belt into the air, I clenched my whole body, crying, waiting to feel the first welt on my bare behind. Often my mother would appear, crying and begging my father not to do it, but he always replied that he had no choice.

Each time that black or brown (depending upon his outfit—he was always color coordinated) belt would loom above me like a snake ready to attack, I would squeeze every inch of my body so tight, hoping that it would help ease the pain and sting of the impending assault. By the second whack, I would just pray for it to end. The first was always the worst, because the initial anticipation was terrifying. After that, my mind and body would go numb.

The number of times that leather met my skin varied based on just how snotty I had been or the mood my dad was in. He was the moody type, so all of us had learned to keep our distance at those times when the slightest thing could turn him into a belt wielding monster.

But my father was still my hero. All I wanted was his love, which I always knew I had, even when he took his belt to me. I was "daddy's little girl" for sure. He and I had an indescribable, special bond, so it was very hard to understand how he could hurt me both physically and emotionally. It made me crave his love and adoration more intensely.

My dad and my brother did not share the same special bond. My brother had that same relationship with my mom, however. It often felt like two teams within one family. So, if I was on Team Dad, *why was I the one being abused more often?* It was because my brother was smart and learned from my mistakes. Of course, he was always able to delay the pain longer than me since he was a skinny little thing who could get himself under, over, up, or down any piece of furniture better than me.

You'd think I would have been relieved those few times when Michael was the target of my dad's rage, but no. If there had been a choice, I would have preferred that I was the victim instead of him. I would cringe with anticipation as my brother made his way into his hiding spot. I would run to my room, close the door, and curl up into a ball on my bed, tightly squeezing my eyes and covering my ears, hoping I wouldn't be able to hear what was about to transpire.

It slightly muffled my brother's pleading cries and my father's screaming, but the sound would stab me in my heart—I just wanted it to end. I would be quietly sobbing in my room as my brother was doing the same in the aftermath of his punishment.

I assumed that this was a regular occurrence in everyone's home, not just mine. I did find a handful of other victims who had been the recipient of the dreaded belt once or twice but not nearly as often as me. I thought maybe I was more of a "bad girl" than my friends. I guess I deserved it because I couldn't control my mouth.

I was ashamed. Ashamed that I wasn't the perfect child. I didn't look or act the way I was supposed to. *What is wrong with me?* I thought to myself. *Why can't I just be like everyone else?*

As the years went by, the belt stayed in the loops of my dad's pants. There was still the occasional slap across the face, which stung like crazy and momentarily left a pink handprint on my face, but no more across the knee. I knew this punishment was a result of generational habits—it's just the way it was in our family. It's what my father knew, so he continued this horrific family tradition.

Well, not me! I knew I would never hurt my children in any way. I made that decision years and years before I became a parent. That type of torture was inhumane, and I vowed that I would at no time be a belt wielding monster.

And I kept that vow. That disgusting family tradition ended with me. I was the last victim.

On second thought... maybe I can!

♥ 6 ♥

I Was Always Afraid This Would Happen

"If you're going through hell, keep going."
—Winston Churchill

I kept my parents high up in the sky on a pedestal. I liked to look at them up there because it was scary for me to think that they didn't have it all figured out. It left me with a feeling of insecurity. I mean if they didn't know what they were doing, and I certainly didn't, we were screwed! There were little glimpses (like my dad hitting me, or my mom hiding food) when I questioned if they were right, but that was because I didn't like their parenting methods. Deep down, I believed that they knew what was best for me, and that someday I would be all-knowing just like them. The moment I discovered my parents weren't perfect was the summer between seventh and eighth grade.

My parents had finally convinced me to attend a sleep away camp. Camp had been the best time of their lives, so they had always wanted me to have the same experience. Unfortunately, I was not them. I was afraid of my own shadow, so leaving my

47

family for eight weeks to live with strangers and sleep in a bunk was not at all appealing. I had attended day camp since I was three years old, and I was fairly happy with this arrangement, but I felt like I was a disappointment to them because I had not carried on the family summer tradition of attending sleep away camp.

A friend of mine had attended a camp in Massachusetts for several years, and she would share stories that made it sound amazing and go on and on about how great it was. She would tell me about all the camp friends she had made who lived in different parts of the Northeast. It did pique my interest a bit, and I figured since it was my responsibility to carry on our family tradition, I might as well take the leap with a friend instead of trying it out on my own.

I tried to back out as my departure date drew near, but our money was non-refundable. My parents told me how great it was going to be as they re-lived their own camp memories with me for the millionth time. When the day finally arrived, I was absolutely petrified. My self-consciousness was on overdrive when I met all the girls in my bunk. I was the only chunky one, *again*. They all had the cutest shorts, halter tops, and bathing suits, while I had my big T-shirts, longer shorts, and bathing suits with a skirt attached.

Most of them were returnees since it was common for most kids to begin going to sleepaway camp around the age of eight or nine. They all knew each other and had a lot of catching up to do, which left me on the outside looking in. Things went downhill from there. I saw the bunk, bathroom, and shower situation and immediately panicked. I needed to figure out how I would be able to undress, shower, dry off, and dress without anyone glimpsing a peak at my naked body. It was not going to be easy, and I contemplated not showering for the summer or showering in the middle of the night when everyone else was sleeping.

The next challenge was the lake. The day camp at home had a swimming pool, but *here* there was no pool. We swam in a lake with creatures, fish, mud, and all things slimy. Getting out of the lake required climbing up a steep ladder. There were two problems with the ladder. The first is it was difficult for me to hoist my plump body out of the gross water and up onto the ladder. The second was that my hips, butt, and thighs were out there on display for all to see. At the pool, I could strategically place my towel right next to the steps, so I could grab it the minute I got out of the water, allowing less than a minute for people to view my body.

A similar towel placement was not possible at the lake. We had to leave our towels up on a hill far from the lake and the ladder. I considered running up the hill, so I could cover up quicker, but then my fat would jiggle while I ran. So instead, I tried to appear cool while taking the walk up the hill to the safety of my towel. Luckily, no one was able to see how I was internally freaking out.

I hated this place and needed to go home. The camp didn't allow you to call home for the first week since there was an adjustment period for newbies and hearing your parents' voices was more upsetting than not speaking to them at all. I made it known to my counselor that I couldn't wait that long. I had to speak to them, and it was urgent. I didn't tell her that the urgent matter was that they had to come and rescue me. Somehow, she convinced the head counselor to let me call. I'm sure all my visits to the nurse, because I always felt sick during swimming, didn't hurt my case either.

I called home, and only my mom was there. She told me my dad was out and that I needed to give camp more time. I sobbed and sobbed and couldn't believe that she wouldn't rescue me. I was completely distraught and needed to get my father on the phone because he was a big softy. The problem was that it was extremely difficult to get anyone to allow me to call home once, let alone twice.

Eventually, all my crying won out. After about two weeks, my parents arrived to pick me up and take me home. I was thrilled, but neither of them looked very pleased. I had so much stuff jammed into the trunk and back seat of the car that I had to sit between my parents on the front bench seat for the four-hour ride home. No one was really speaking and there was an uncomfortable feeling in the air. My eyes darted back and forth, taking turns looking at each of them for a clue as to what was going on.

At first, I assumed that they were angry at me for making such a stink and possibly losing some of their money. I questioned them repeatedly, and they both quickly told me that they understood, and all was fine. The four-hour ride felt more like four days. I fantasized about getting out of the car, going into the house, seeing Chuckles, and going to my own room where I could relax and be by myself. I would be free to put on whatever clothes felt comfortable without others watching me.

The cramped, endless journey finally ended, and I did just as I had fantasized except for the lock myself in my room part. Chuckles and Michael greeted me, and they were both clearly glad to see me. *At least someone was happy I was home!* A few minutes later, my dad said they needed to talk to us, and we should all go sit in the living room. *Sit in the living room?* That was an odd request since the living room was typically off limits—unless it was a holiday and we had company. The minute my father uttered the request, I immediately started asking, "What's going on? What do we need to discuss?"

Tears started welling up in my father's eyes before any words came out of his mouth. *Oh no! Someone must have died.* All my grandparents were alive, so I was terrified that he was going to tell us that something had happened to one of them. *It had to be that. Why else would my dad be crying?*

Well, after the words came tumbling out of his mouth I almost (but not really) wished I had been right. He said that he and my mom were going to separate, and he would be moving out. I asked if it was for good, and he said he didn't know. He gave some grown up nonsense explanation about relationships going through difficult times, yada, yada … I was no longer listening. All four of us were crying, and each of my parents explained this had nothing to do with us—that they loved us very much and that would never change.

I had a million questions. "Where are you going to live?" I asked.

My father replied, "I'll be staying at your Aunt Judy's house."

"Aunt Judy's house? But she lives so far away … in New Jersey."

"I know it's far, but I'll drive out here to see you on weekends."

"When will this happen?" I choked out between sobs.

"Now."

Just an hour ago, my biggest concern was how much longer it would take for us to pull into our driveway. Boy, how I wish I could turn back time. Camp was looking like a fantasy land after this nightmare that I just stepped into.

One of my biggest fears had always been that my parents would get divorced. I had always felt so badly for my friends who didn't live with both parents. As I would listen to their stories about holidays and weekends and the tension that existed between them all, I would silently pray *please never let this happen to me.*

Clearly, I hadn't prayed correctly or often enough. My dad was leaving us.

As Dad headed upstairs to pack, I ran after him crying, begging, and pleading for him not to leave. Once it became clear he was leaving, I asked him to take me with him. After all, I always loved being with my aunt and cousins, I could move there with him. Naturally, he told me that couldn't happen. I was shot down again. I watched his every move as if to memorize this moment. I helped him transfer his perfectly color coordinated socks into his suitcase. I followed him into the bathroom where he went to retrieve his toiletries.

I was breathing deeply, smelling all his wonderful scents. I sat there remembering how I used to sit on the toilet seat, lid down, and watch while he shaved. I knew each and every step and the wonderful smells that drifted over to me when he applied his shaving cream, after shave lotion and cologne. I would breathe in comfort, love, and safety while sharing those precious moments together.

Those days were over.

How could this be happening?

Michael and I perched on our knees on the living room couch watching longingly through the large glass window as my dad packed up his car and drove away. I now turned my attention to my mom. *Was she happy about this? Is this what she wanted?*

I found her on her bed, crying. Instead of questioning her, I snuggled against her and cried along with her, stunned that I had any tears left inside of me. In the aftermath of our emotional embrace, I did ask her what the real story was. She stuck to the "company" line, explaining how these things sometimes happen, even though no one wants them to.

While listening with one ear, my mind drifted back to a few moments from the past few months. I do remember my parents fighting but that happened occasionally. I mean, everyone argues now and then. I had also come across my mother sitting at the kitchen table one night, in the dark, quietly crying. When I questioned her, she didn't really have much to say, so I had shrugged it off and had turned my attention back to my own stuff.

I was still laying with my mom when the phone rang, and I picked up the receiver. My dad was on the other end. He wanted us to know he had arrived safely. I asked him if he had re-thought his decision during his ride across the Verrazano Bridge, but the answer was no. Our conversation was short, and he told me he would call me tomorrow. When I hung up, my mom told me that Aunt Natalie (her sister-in-law) would be coming to stay with us for a few hours, while my mom and my uncle went out for a bit.

I didn't think the day could become any more bizarre, but it had. First of all, my aunt and uncle never came over unannounced. Secondly, my aunt had never babysat us. *What could my mom and her brother possibly be doing together on a Saturday night without my aunt?*

It was awkward because my aunt was a bit odd, and we really didn't have a relationship with her—other than saying hello and goodbye when we would get together with them on holidays or the occasional Sunday. I did question her, seeing if I could get her to break. She mentioned that my mom and uncle were going to see my dad, which made absolutely no sense since only a few hours had passed since he abandoned us. I was absolutely clueless, and at this point was too emotionally and physically exhausted to ask any more questions. But as hard as I tried, I couldn't stay awake long enough for my mother to return. My curiosity had to wait until morning to finally learn the truth.

My father was having an affair. My mother wasn't the one to tell me, instead, she had me call my dad, so he could tell me himself. I thought for sure that no day could ever be as bad as the previous one, but I was wrong. This was completely and utterly devastating. My dad didn't love his family enough to

54

stay faithful to us. He had found a woman who lived in New Jersey, and who had a ten-year-old daughter.

My dad had left me.

Of course, he assured me that this wasn't the case, and that he loved me more than anything. Now *he* was the one pleading and begging. Pleading and begging for me to believe him and try and understand. At first, I didn't. I couldn't. And then I decided that this was all my mom's fault. She had driven him away and into the arms of another woman.

I verbally assaulted my mother with accusations and made her cry, but I didn't care. She was responsible for this mess. I felt like I had to fix it. I was the only one who *could* fix it. I would convince each of them to give it another try. I succeeded.

A week later my dad was back home. It was scary and awkward, like we were all strangers living together for the first time. We were all walking on eggshells and not able to let our guards down and be ourselves. I was always upbeat and trying to keep the peace but a few weeks later, my dad moved out again.

Simultaneously, my Bat Mitzvah was approaching. I had been preparing (you need to learn prayers that are specific to the date of your event) and was excited about the service and the party that would follow, where all my friends and family would gather together to celebrate with food, music, and dancing. Most of my fellow Hebrew-school classmates had already had their celebrations. Mine was one of the last because your date is based on your birthday.

After the second separation, my father informed me that he and my mom thought it would be best if we postponed my date. *POSTPONED? That's not fair! How would that even work? Would I have to wait until my fourteenth birthday?* He told me that it would be prior to my fourteenth birthday, and we would work out all the details with the Rabbi. He explained that based on the current situation with him and my mom, my Bat Mitzvah would be an uncomfortable, impossible day for everyone. I asked what would be different in a few months, and he assured me that we would have figured it out by then.

It's not like I had a choice. The decision was already made. I would soon learn that the hard part would be scheduling a new date. In our synagogue, almost every Saturday was booked with Bar and Bat Mitzvahs two years in advance. No one canceled, except for me. So, the only way to make it work was to have my ceremony on a Friday night in June and the party the next day.

I wasn't even a teenager yet, and my life had suddenly become very complicated. I had the responsibility of keeping our family together, which was not an easy task. Over the next six months, my dad moved in and out one more time until he moved back in permanently. It took many months for all of us to adjust. Every time I left the house, I was afraid to come home, fearful that my parents would have separated, yet again.

As time went on, and my dad remained at home, my anxiety eased up. I was able to get on with my life, especially now that I was a grownup middle schooler. My attention shifted to my friends and my own life, but I was a changed girl. I had discovered the truth about my parents, more specifically my dad. He was not perfect. My safe, small world had been turned upside down.

My knight in shining armor had fallen off his horse.

On second thought... maybe I can!

♥ 7 ♥

Always a Bridesmaid

"What we think, we become." —Buddha

Well, fifth and sixth graders certainly weren't getting married back in the early 70's, but they were beginning to feel that fluttery, exciting, and scary feeling of having a crush. I didn't flit from crush to crush like most girls my age. No siree, I was one loyal girl! When I fell for someone, I was all in. I wasn't a quitter. I believed if I was able to hang on long enough the boy would come around and see me for who I really was underneath my thick body.

My first crush (not including David Cassidy, my forever crush) was in fifth grade. His name was Gene, and he had reddish brown hair. Gene was smart, athletic, and funny—a triple threat! I would blush whenever he looked my way, even though I knew he wasn't looking at me. I sat on the other side of the room since his last name began with an "E" and mine with a "S," so, I rarely got a chance to talk to him. I admired him from afar and drew hearts inside my notebook where no one else could see. Inside the hearts it would always say

"Debbie + Gene." Sometimes, I would draw cupid arrows coming out of the heart, and other times I would write "Debbie + Gene 4ever."

I studied Gene like my life depended on it. I knew where he lived, how he walked to school, who he talked to, and most importantly, which girls he was paying attention to. I would lay in my bed and dream about the day when Gene would come to his senses and realize that the perfect girl was right under his nose. Of course, I was the perfect girl or at least the perfect girl for him. If I noticed him flirting with someone, my day and night would be ruined. I would cry and fantasize about the day that he would come running into my arms. Deep down I knew that would never happen because popular boys like Gene (especially those who were a triple threat) certainly wouldn't be paying attention to a chubby, unpopular girl like me.

When I began playing on sports teams in sixth grade and hanging out with the more popular, athletic crowd, I figured my odds had improved. However, I soon discovered that Gene's eyes seemed to be transfixed on a girl who had the perfect body. She was slim but athletic, and her shapely legs looked so long in her shorts that they would turn any boy's head. My tree stump legs were no match, and I lost Gene to another woman.

Junior high school was the beginning of my obsessive crushes. Frank was my first obsession. Since I was a newbie, my crush lasted only for a year. I was still an amateur. Frank had a great personality and a wonderful sense of humor. I hadn't gone to elementary school with him, so I hoped that maybe he wouldn't notice my body.

He and I got along splendidly. We were in some of the same classes and sat close to each other. We would whisper and laugh. It was obvious that he liked me, and it was only a matter of time until he acted on it. Life was looking up. Forget about Gene, I had found my man. Frank was even best friends with my best friend's boyfriend, so the four of us would hang out fairly often. If he wasn't around, I would casually try to ask his friend where he was because I didn't want to give myself and my crush away. I heard it was better to be mysterious and play hard to get. The problem was that everyone could read me like an open book. I was unable to hide my goo-goo eyes and longing gaze each time Frank spoke to me. The whole world seemed to know how I felt about Frank, including Frank. Talk about utter and total embarrassment!

If Frank knew, then why wasn't he doing anything about it? I would have been up for a game of spin the bottle with just him. Next thing I knew, Frank was talking about other girls to me. *Oh, so that's how it was going to be?* I was his confidant. I figured I would play along until he got sick of all those other girls. Frank would one day have his "AHA" moment and see that he and I were destined to be together. To make sure that day arrived, I would need to play along, listen to him talk about other girls and be his buddy.

It was absolute torture playing this little game. It was even worse when Frank would "ask a girl out," which meant you were an official couple. Now instead of it being the four of us hanging out, we became an uneven group of five. Everyone wanted to play a game in the dark, but clearly that didn't interest me. *What was I supposed to do alone in the dark?* I felt absolutely, positively pathetic. It was so clear to me that Frank and I got along so much better than he did with those other girls, so why was he with them and not me? I was starting to see a pattern.

While seventh grade was all about Frank, eighth grade was all about Bobby and John. John had been my next-door neighbor for my entire life. We grew up in a middle-class neighborhood, where our houses were close enough to look through each other's kitchen windows and see when we were eating dinner. John was two years older than me, and he was tall, athletic, and cute. He and I never really spoke. When we were younger, all the kids in the neighborhood would play kick ball, stoop ball, and ringolevio together. In those days, we would spend countless hours and days playing, riding bikes, and "calling" (ringing the doorbell and asking if your friend was home) on each other to come out and play.

I would never "call" on John. We just didn't have that type of relationship. He was older and had this air of "coolness" (like The Fonz) about him. John played baseball, but his real passion was boating and fishing. We grew up on Long Island, so water was never very far away. John began hanging around with Bobby, a boy who lived around the block who was my age. Bobby and I went to elementary school together but had nothing to do with one another. He was a bit odd, not as smart as me and hung out with a different crowd, so I really didn't know him. John and Bobby shared a love of boating and fishing and worked together at a boatyard.

I had my own group of girlfriends who would often come over after school. My house was always the gathering place, since I had a mom who worked and didn't get home until 5:30 p.m. This meant we had an unsupervised house to hang out in. The only issue was my brother Michael. He was very astute. He perfected the art of bribery at a young age. The minute we were doing something bad, like breaking into my parents' liquor cabinet, I would hear Michael say, "I'm telling." Now the bargaining game would begin, where I would offer him something to keep quiet and he would ask for more. He was a master negotiator, and it would cost me a pretty penny to buy his silence. Sometimes, my friends would have to cough up a little money too. After all, the financial burden shouldn't just be on me.

If John were around, he would scare and threaten Michael (in the nicest way possible), and we wouldn't have to pay. My friends and I would hang out in my front yard, so we might run into John and Bobby. Many of my friends had a crush on John since he was an elusive high school boy. We all began hanging out together at my house. My home turned into a brothel each day between 3–5:30 pm., and I was the Madam. John and Bobby had it made because the girls outnumbered them by four to one. They had the pick of the litter, and I was the one who would make the deal. The process began when either of the boys or one of the girls would start talking more often. Most commonly, a goofy face would accompany the conversation. Once the clock struck 5:15 p.m., everyone would disperse. Then after dinner the phone chain would begin.

All evening I would be on the phone discussing the events of that day and playing matchmaker. My friends would call me and ask if their crush liked them, and we would analyze every detail before reaching a conclusion. If there was consensus that the person liked them back, I would ask on their behalf. It was a tough decision, as I didn't want to embarrass anyone. If I got a positive response, the couple would feel confident enough to approach each other. But when they started dating, it was awkward for me because I was left alone, always longing to be part of a couple.

When my harem of friends was not around, John, Bobby, and I would hang out. We always had a great time. They gave me the nickname "Derb" and the three of us grew really close. I was just "one of the guys." *What else was new?* There was a time when I had a crush on Bobby but just like with Frank, there was always a cuter, thinner girl he had his eye on. This pattern continued for a year or so until we all grew more mature and were high schoolers.

My longest boy obsession began when I was thirteen years old. I had a major crush on Joan's (my BFF since the age of twelve) brother, Paul. He was only a year older, and we got along incredibly well. We always had something to talk and laugh about. Sometimes I would call Joan, and if Paul answered the phone, I might never even get to talk to Joan because he and I would speak for hours. It would also happen occasionally when I was at their house, hanging out or sleeping over. Understandably, Joan would get annoyed. I know there were times when she felt like I was only there to see and talk to Paul. This certainly wasn't true, but it was a great bonus!

As always, I wore my feelings on my sleeve, and everyone knew I had a crush on Paul, including, but not limited to, Paul and his whole family. Everyone was cringing behind my back as they watched me make a fool of myself time and time again. But I was not one to quit. *Paul liked me, that was clear, so why didn't he like me in THAT way?* Once again, there could only be one answer. The fat girl never gets the guy, but it certainly wasn't from lack of trying.

Each year there was a Sadie Hawkins dance where the girl had to ask the guy to be her date. There was only one person that I would ask, and everyone knew who it was. I kept trying to figure out how and when I would muster up the courage to make my move. I tried to work up the courage to ask Paul. I would tell myself it was go time, but then a reason presented itself that made it an inopportune time. Finally, it came down to the wire. The dance was just days away, and I had to act swiftly. I swore to myself that I just had to do it.

On *the* day, I tried to pop the question while we were at his house. I don't know if Joan warned her brother, or he just knew it was coming. But it was clear he was avoiding me by swiftly walking from room to room, telling me he had to get ready to go out. He ran out the door, and I ran after him yelling at him to please stop because I needed to talk to him.

I chased Paul for blocks and blocks and blocks. I kept yelling and he kept laughing and running. I'm guessing he thought I would eventually give up or pass out from running for so long and hard, but I didn't do either. I was proud to say that I had made a commitment to myself, and I was going to see this through. Eventually, he realized he wasn't getting out of this, so he stopped, and I blurted out the big question. He squirmed and told me that he wasn't really into going to dances. I tried to convince him that it would be fun. I mean after all, he called me "Disco Deb," and we danced to Donna Summer's "Bad Girls" in his living room, so why wouldn't we enjoy a dance? There was nothing left to do but accept his answer, turn around, and walk back the mile to Paul and Joan's house to tell Joan what had happened.

A few days later I found out that another girl had asked Paul to the dance, and he agreed to go. I felt dumb, humiliated, and embarrassed. *Why did I think that he would ever be seen in public with me? This is what I get for putting myself out there.* I never went to that dance. All my friends and their dates went, and I stayed home and cried my eyes out while eating ice cream and Oreos. It just wasn't fair. I couldn't help but loathe myself.

My Paul crush lasted for three years but never amounted to anything other than friendship. Even the fact that I put in the time and effort to win him over had made no difference. I thought he might crack with my perseverance, but he was a tough one.

Many of my male friends throughout the years only saw me as a friend. It didn't matter how much they enjoyed spending time with me or how great my personality was. Being a chubby girl was just not cool. It would be considered social suicide for them to pursue anything more than a friendship with me. So, I was left to dream of the day when either a boy would come to their senses, or I would find a way to become skinny, which was easier said than done.

Despite having many friends, I felt hopeless about finding love. Being overweight made me feel unlovable and the thought of being physically intimate was out of the question. I feared showing my body to anyone and resigned myself to the idea of becoming an "old maid" to avoid facing my insecurities.

However, deep down, I knew I was lying to myself. I longed to be part of a couple and held onto the hope that someday my dream would come true.

On second thought... maybe I can!

♥ 8 ♥

Softball Tryouts

"If you hear a voice within you say, 'you cannot paint,' then by all means paint and that voice will be silenced."
—Vincent Van Gogh

Softball was always my favorite and best sport. I was a pitcher and first baseman. I was a decent batter, a slow runner, and naturally *not* a base stealer. I had some confidence in my ability but certainly not enough to believe that I could make it in the big leagues—you know, high school! Our high school had approximately 2,000 students in just three grades (ninth grade was in the junior high building). *What are the chances that I would be one of the girls to make the softball team?*

Stacy was a friend of mine who was an excellent athlete. She excelled in every area of most sports, but she was not socially confident or outgoing. I think she and I had an unspoken understanding that we both knew what it was like to not fit in but for very different reasons. She spent hours, days, and weeks trying to convince me to attend the softball tryouts when we were in tenth grade. She would practice with me and compliment me on my skills. For a minute, she had me thinking that maybe I *did* have a chance of making the team.

Instead of remaining positive, I had a nightmare that played over and over in my mind. The girls and the coaches would be looking down their noses, laughing and talking behind my back when I came up to bat or was having a catch. They were all thinking how ridiculous it was that I even showed up thinking I could possibly be a part of the high school team. I was certainly not interested in, once again, being the butt of others' jokes just because of my weight or lack of athletic ability.

Tryouts were a four-day ordeal, and at 7 a.m. on the fifth day, they would post the names of the girls who had made the team on a bulletin board outside the gym for all to see. The whole idea was nauseating to me, but Stacy was persistent and believed in me. After all, she was a star athlete and would know a loser when she saw one. Even though my head screamed not to do it, my heart won out. The day the tryouts began I could hardly hold my nerves in check during the school day. Stacy accompanied me to the tryout, and she was my partner when we began warming up and having a catch. Catching and throwing were strengths of mine, so I was beginning to relax a bit.

Okay, maybe this wouldn't be so bad. I carefully checked out the competition and thought maybe I wasn't out of my mind for thinking my dream of being on the team would come true. That was until the end of the second day, when they told us that the next day we would be running and sliding. *Did someone say running? sliding? I'm out!*

I had never slid into a base before. For several years, sliding was not allowed in the leagues I played, so I never had to worry about it. There was no way that I was throwing my body on the ground for all to see. *What if my shirt came out and they saw my skin? What if I broke my arm or my leg because I had too much weight to drag to the ground? What if I hurt myself?* Sliding was completely out of the question. *Who needed to play softball? I'm sure there are other, safer things I could do.* The decision was made, I was done with softball and did not return to the tryouts for days three and four—much to Stacy's dismay.

I lived close enough to walk to high school, and every day I would cut through a very large hole in a metal fence that would leave me out onto the school's track. I would have to walk a little more than halfway around the track to get up to the path that led into the school. By day five, I had resigned myself to the fact that softball would no longer be a part of my life. I had actually forgotten that today was the day that the names would be posted.

It was a foggy, chilly April morning as I stepped onto the track just like I did every morning at 7 a.m. I saw someone starting to walk out of the school and head towards me on the track. I assumed the girl had changed her mind and decided not to go to school that day. A minute later, the figure was running towards me, and I realized it was Stacy. She was yelling something, but I couldn't hear what she was saying. Then I remembered that the results were going to be posted today. I assumed she was excited to tell me that she had made the varsity team, instead of junior varsity where most sophomores would be placed.

As she got closer, I could hear her yelling, "Deb, you made the team!" *Excuse me?* I looked over my shoulder to see if another Deb was behind me. I was utterly shocked and confused, and I told her that it was a really cruel joke. Now she and I were eye to eye. "Your name is on the JV list."

"How could that be?" I asked. I missed half the tryout. I had to see this with my own eyes. She led me over to the board and there it was, my name was really on the list! The smile that broke out on my face was as wide as the Grand Canyon as tears of joy trickled down my face.

All the while Stacy was saying, "You did it! You did it!"

Wow. I really did do it!

❤ 9 ❤

Bobby

"The first time you fall in love, it changes you forever, and no matter how hard you try, that feeling just never goes away." –Nicholas Sparks

The summer of 1980, when I was sixteen years old, my life shifted. I stepped WAY out of my comfort zone and attended a seven-week summer program for rising high school seniors at Cornell University. We lived in dorms and attended class, just as if we were already college students. Being the world's biggest scaredy cat, it was totally out of character for me to agree to something like this, but I did it with both trepidation and excitement.

Only, I was not prepared for dorm living and sharing a room with a stranger. Worse yet, a stranger who wound up being a nymphomaniac and would constantly lock me out of the room when she had a visitor—which was constantly. When we were in the room together and it was time for me to change my clothes, I had to maneuver myself in odd ways, so that she wouldn't see any part of my naked body. She, on the other hand, enjoyed parading around naked. Naked! *Seriously?* I didn't know where to look as she would sit on her bed, cross-legged talking to me. Seeing her cute, little naked body just made me feel even worse about my own.

I soon discovered that the other torture chamber, housed in the dorm, was the community bathroom. Now, not only did I have to figure out how to hide myself from my roommate but also from all the other girls on the floor. I would bring so much paraphernalia into the bathroom just so I could make sure every body part was covered when I had to dress or undress. Despite having just showered, I found myself profusely sweating as I tried to deftly maneuver my body and the towel, determined to avoid any potential embarrassment.

The third thing that made this experience difficult for me was the dining hall. Others would be watching and judging everything I put in my mouth, so I felt like I could hardly eat anything. I was a very picky eater, so most of the time, there was nothing there that I even wanted to eat other than ice cream. I lived for seven weeks on salad. There was a salad bar, so I would create the same salad every day, twice a day. In the beginning, I was constantly starving and miserable but as my clothes started to get baggy and my legs started to shrink, I was pleased.

I came home seven weeks later as a new person. I was twenty-five pounds thinner, and I was more confident since I had just lived as a college student—on my own for the summer. None of my friends could say the same. Clearly, I was much more mature now, and high school seemed like it was for babies. Months before, my best friend Joan and my neighbor John had started dating, but this was different from the eighth-grade version of "dating." This was the real thing, and they were in love. Bobby and I would often be with them since they were our respective best friends. We always had a great time, just as we had since eighth grade.

The night I came home from Cornell and the four of us went out, something felt different and almost uncomfortable. I was picking up an unfamiliar vibe from Bobby. He seemed to be looking at and treating me differently. I thought I was hallucinating from lack of nutrition. But after consuming several alcoholic beverages, he kissed me, causing all doubts to fly out of my head. It was my first kiss, and we were laying down on the grass at a park, overlooking the bay at 1 a.m. As we kissed, I was scared that I wasn't doing it right or that he would touch me and feel one of the rolls on my body. I thought he was going to jump up in disgust when he felt a bulge or my "Big Bertha" hips. When I allowed myself to relax and stop thinking, it was one of the best moments of my life.

Joan and I went home to my house that night to find my father on the front lawn, yelling at all of us because it was so late, but even my father's anger couldn't bring me down. The excitement I was feeling had me floating on air. It had finally happened to me! Someone liked me enough to actually kiss me! After I came down from the clouds, I wondered if it was only because he had had something to drink. Maybe when he saw me again in daylight and was completely sober, he would reconsider.

Much to my surprise, that didn't happen. Soon, Bobby and I officially became a couple. I was one-half of a pair. Now I had to figure out how to move forward with our relationship while fully clothed. In the beginning, all that was necessary was unbuttoning or unzippering, not removing, and I was learning to deal with that. Over the next couple of months, I became much more secure in our relationship and Bobby's feelings for me. I eventually took the plunge and lost my virginity in a very dark room under a lot of covers. I felt like I had officially become a desirable woman.

Bobby and I were together every spare second of the day. I was no longer interested in hanging out with my friends or playing softball. I always wanted to be with Bobby because he made me feel loved, desirable, and special. Joan and John were still a couple and the four of us had wonderful adventures together on John's boat and on the beach. We went to bars and movies together; my world couldn't have been any better.

The only little, nagging issue was that intellectually, Bobby and I were not at the same level. Now please don't misunderstand what I'm saying. I'm no genius, and my conversations were not super deep by any means. However, Bobby would say things that I felt were downright dumb. If we were around other people (excluding Joan and John), I would put him down or correct him because I was embarrassed.

However, he had his own talents. He was incredibly handy and was a wonderful wood craftsman. He had a lot of practical skills, and I had none. We both excelled in different areas but for some reason I felt that his intelligence, or my skewed view of his intelligence, was something I would be judged for. People would think that I had to "settle" for him because "no smart man would want a chubby girl like me." I forgot to mention that the weight I had lost that summer found me again in a matter of weeks. By that time, Bobby and I had fallen in love, so he didn't seem to care that my body had expanded.

One night the four of us (Joan, John, Bobby, and I) were hanging out at Joan's and the conversation turned to food. Jokingly, Bobby coined the term "Pure Debbie Pound Cake." John and Joan thought it was hysterical and decided that this would be my new nickname. I, however, did not think this was funny. In fact, I was devastated that these three people, who I loved and cared about, could be so cruel. We were practically adults (seventeen and nineteen years old). I thought at this point in my life I would no longer be the butt of any more fat jokes. Bobby was supposed to love me, but his nickname revealed how he truly saw me. I was just a big poundcake to him.

Why me?
Why did this curse never seem to go away?
What did I ever do to deserve this?

It was hard enough hanging out with three skinny people most of the time, especially in the summer when we were constantly at the beach or on the boat. Joan would be sunbathing in her bikinis, and I would see Bobby take a look, then act like he was looking at something else. Even this person who pledged his undying love to me knew that in the end, I was worthless because I was just a fat girl.

I cried for hours that night once I was alone in my bed. There was a pain in my heart that I had never felt before. I had believed Bobby loved me for *me*. He knew how much my weight bothered me and instead of honoring and understanding my feelings, he had exploited them. The hurt I felt was much different than all the other countless times in my life when I had been called names. *How could he really love me and be so cruel?* I questioned him once we were alone. He apologized and told me he was just trying to make Joan and John laugh. In my mind, I had no choice but to forgive him and move on. After all, I finally had a boyfriend. I couldn't risk losing what might be my only chance at love.

Our relationship continued to grow. We were inseparable. Bobby was always at my house. He became part of the family. Even my grandparents, aunts, uncles, and cousins knew him well. He would often be there to celebrate holidays with us and was very fun, easy going, confident, and cheerful around us.

The idea of leaving him to go off to college at the end of the school year was too much to bear. Bobby had become my partner. We were a team, a pair, a couple. I couldn't imagine living life without him. All the confidence I had gained at Cornell was long gone and I didn't want to go away to college. I wanted to remain home safely in the arms of a boy who loved me, but I felt I would regret it. I had career plans to become an attorney for professional athletes so staying at home would not be the correct path.

In the end, Bobby and I devised a plan where I could pursue the career of my dreams, while still maintaining our relationship. We needed to attend the same college; however,

Bobby was not as good a student as I was, which made it difficult to land in the same location. We both applied to Penn State, and I was accepted to the main campus at State College, PA but he wasn't. Instead, Bobby was accepted at a satellite location, which was three hours away from where I would be. Eventually, assuming he kept his grades up, he would be able to transfer to the main campus, and we could be together.

The plan wasn't ideal, but we would make it work. Bobby would have his car and be able to see me whenever he could. We were ready to move forward, but still had many months together before beginning our college journeys. We made sure to spend each and every moment having fun and making wonderful memories together. Life was starting to look up.

On second thought... maybe I can!

♥ 10 ♥

Strike #4

"You never know how strong you are until being strong is your only choice." –Bob Marley

How many times in your life have you heard the phrase "your life can change in an instant"? You hear it with your ears, but do you ever stop to process it? Or do you think it doesn't really apply to you—only to other people? When you're a teenager you think a life changing event is your friend dropping you or, on a positive note, the boy you had a crush on asking you out. Totally life changing!

I certainly never thought that it would *actually* happen to me—until it did.

It was the day after I graduated from high school. I had been lying around all day in my parents' bed watching TV, while they were both at work. My mom worked locally, and my dad took the train into New York City each day. That afternoon my dad had called to check on me, as he often did. We had a brief conversation, and he went back to work while I returned to watching reruns. In the early evening while my mom was preparing dinner, the phone rang. I picked up the phone and heard my mom pick up the downstairs extension as I was saying hello. I was greeted by a woman I had never spoken to before, and I assumed she was calling to speak to my mom. I was just about to hang up and roll back over when I heard the woman say that my father was sitting at her kitchen table. *Who the heck is this woman and why is my dad in her house?*

She went on to explain that he appeared to be drunk but was able to remember his phone number. He had sideswiped her parked car, then rang her doorbell to apologize and make arrangements to have it fixed. It had become apparent that he was not in his right mind and should not get back in the car and drive home, so she suggested my mom come and get him. I hung up the phone and ran down the stairs as my mom was still on with the stranger, writing down her address.

My mom yelled at me to get in the car because I would need to drive one of the cars home. Braless, in old sweatpants, and with matted hair, I jumped into the passenger seat of my mom's car. I started asking her questions that she did not know the answer to, so we discussed the possibilities. First, it was highly unusual for my dad to be drunk. That's not to say he didn't enjoy his gin and tonics because he did. He had been known to have one or two during a lunch business meeting, which they seemed to do a lot back then (think *Mad Men*, although this was 1981).

Earlier that day, both of us had talked to him, and he was fine. Maybe he met a friend on the train, and they went to the bar car, which if you're not familiar with the term, each train would have a car that had a bar and tables. I remember walking through the smoke-filled train car as a little girl and hating all the smells and looks of people who were sitting in there. However, this scenario would also be unlikely since my dad would not get behind the wheel if he was drunk.

Moving on to the next hypothesis, we discussed the symptoms of having a heart attack. Neither of us believed that someone with heart issues would appear to be intoxicated but what did we know? At the time, I was seventeen and my mom was only thirty-nine, so luckily, we didn't have much experience with illness.

We pulled into the driveway, jumped out of the car, and rang the bell. The woman led us to where my father sat at her kitchen table. He was slurring his words and truly did appear to be drunk. We asked if he had had a drink, and he said that he had one drink at lunch, which had been seven hours earlier. My mom thanked the woman and helped my dad get into her car while I jumped into his car to drive home. I was left all alone, my mind still searching for answers. *At least he didn't appear to be in any kind of pain or distress*, I thought. *It's such a hot day, so maybe he's dehydrated*. I convinced myself that once he got home, had a drink of water, and changed out of his business suit, he would feel much better.

When I pulled into the driveway, my mom was already leading my dad to the couch in the den, and she yelled at me to run and get Dr. Green. My parents' doctor lived two doors down from us. There was something about him that I didn't like. It wasn't that I disliked him, but I didn't get a warm and fuzzy feeling from him—I'm all about the warm and fuzzy.

As I ran to his front door, I tried to work up the courage to actually ring the bell. I was cursing my mother in my head for asking me to do this instead of Michael, although Michael wasn't even home. After all, she knows how shy and insecure I am. *Maybe Dr. Green would be angry that I was bothering him at dinnertime. Maybe he would yell at me for disturbing him and tell us to go to the hospital. Maybe he or any of his family members wouldn't be home, and then I wouldn't have to talk to anyone.*

As I tried to work up the courage to ring the bell, I told myself that I had to do this for my dad. It could be important that he see the doctor, so I had to give it a try even though I really, really, really didn't want to do it! I had to be brave and muster up enough courage to press the button.

My heart was beating out of my chest as one of the doctor's teenage sons answered the door. The words just spilled out so quickly it was amazing that he understood me. As I was still talking, the son started yelling for his dad. The doctor appeared with his black doctor bag, just like *Marcus Welby, M.D.* and stepped out of the door. He began speed walking towards my house, and I stood shoulder to shoulder with him, telling him everything that had happened.

We found my dad lying on the couch with his eyes closed. The doctor tried to rouse him, saying, "Larry, Larry, get up."

My dad groggily opened his eyes and greeted the doctor with a very slurred, "Hi, what are you doing here?" The doctor then grabbed his shoulder while giving him the command to sit up. He asked my dad to describe what had happened, and he seemed to recall getting off the train and into his car. He then said that he must have sneezed and lost control of the wheel and hit the parked car.

While this was happening, my mom and I stood there observing. So many thoughts were simultaneously looping in my brain. With each response my dad gave, it was a clue for me to decipher if this was going to be a big deal or not. It seemed to me that if this was a major medical emergency, my dad wouldn't be capable of sitting and talking, so I was cautiously optimistic.

The doctor then pivoted to ask ridiculously obvious questions. "What year is it?"

"1981," my dad replied.

"Who is the president?"

"Ronald Regan," my dad responded.

"Where are we?"

"In my house."

Okay, I thought. *This is going extremely well*—until it wasn't. The next order my father received was to stand up. The doctor was on my dad's left and my mom on his right. Each of them reached under my dad's armpits to hoist him to his feet. They went to let go and my dad almost fell to the floor. The doctor quickly ordered my mom to help him back to the couch and call 9-1-1. He muttered something about a stroke. *A stroke? Is this doctor a quack or what?* I never liked him and maybe that's why. *Only very old people have strokes, didn't he know this?* My dad's forty-sixth birthday was only a few days away. *Forty-six-year-olds don't have strokes, so why did he even mention this word?*

But panic overtook every pore of my body. *9-1-1? Why? My dad had gotten 100% on his quiz, so shouldn't that be a good thing?*

Maybe he fell because he's tired. Everything became a blur. I heard the sirens and four paramedics running into our house with a stretcher. I was literally living my worst nightmare. I begged and pleaded with God to please let my dad be okay. *He doesn't deserve this, he's so young.* It wasn't until I saw my dad surrounded by men with medical devices, being quickly attended to that it crossed my mind, he might die. With tears welling up in my eyes, I watched in disbelief, almost like I was floating from the ceiling looking down and watching this all happen. I stood there paralyzed in fear. I never saw them load the stretcher that held the one man in this world who loved me unconditionally.

My mother's voice jarred me back to reality as she was running out the door into her car to follow the ambulance to the hospital. She told me to meet her there, so I grabbed my keys and followed her out the door to get into my own white, 1980 Ford Mustang. The sun was still shining, but I had trouble seeing the road through the puddles of water that were quickly forming in my eyes. The puddles quickly progressed to a sea of sobs accompanied by loud noises and screams. I was stopped at a light when I noticed that people were staring at me through their car windows. The person who stopped in the lane next to me was kind enough to mouth the words "are you okay?" I shook my head and regained my composure as the light turned green.

The last thing I wanted to do was draw any attention to myself. I hadn't made much progress in that area since the early days of elementary school. My mom had missed the red light, so she was ahead of me, and I was unable to see the direction she was heading. I had never driven to the hospital before, so I wasn't exactly sure where it was, so a bit of panic began to set in yet again.

As I finally drove up to the hospital, I sighed so loud that the whole hospital probably heard me. My anxiety kicked up several notches as I approached the entrance to the emergency department. *What if I can't find my mom? What if this wasn't where I was supposed to go? Would I need to actually ask someone for help?* New, scary questions continued to pop into my brain every second.

I spotted my mother sitting on a yellow chair that was attached to a row of other chairs. It looked like a bench but with individual bucket seats of yellow and orange. She sat there crying into her cupped hands. I ran over to her and sat in the orange seat next to hers, and we sat and waited and waited and waited. Each time the big doors that led down a restricted hallway swung open, we both, in unison, turned our heads to see if it was someone coming out to speak to us. It seemed that several days and nights passed before a doctor emerged and called our last name.

We got up and ran over to him almost tackling the poor guy. He then delivered the news. My dad had suffered a massive stroke and it was a miracle that he had survived. It was still touch and go, so he would remain in the intensive care unit (ICU) until he was stable. My mom fired off questions like she was shooting off an automatic weapon. The doctor explained how the stroke was the size of a small grapefruit, located in the right side of his brain, which meant that the left side of his body had been affected. His symptoms had worsened since his arrival, and now he was unable to move his left arm or leg. It was too early to say whether the paralysis was permanent or not. He allowed my mom to go see my dad for just a few minutes but not both of us.

As I watched my mother disappear through the big, scary hospital doors, I tried to envision what my dad looked like on the other side. My father was paralyzed. *What did paralyzed mean? Wheelchair bound for the rest of his life?* My dad loved physical activity. He had been a basketball and baseball player as a kid and young adult. He and my mom loved to dance, bowl, and play tennis. His love of movement was his lifeline, his outlet, his identity.

I turned away from the doors that led to my paralyzed father and ran into the phone booth that stood in the corner of the lobby. I dug through the bottom of my purse searching for a dime, so I could call Bobby. He was my rock, and I needed him desperately. I hated calling his house because I was very uncomfortable speaking to his parents, but today was different from any other day in my life. I deposited the coin in the thin slot, waited to hear it reach the bottom and dialed Bobby's number. His mom answered. I quickly said hello and asked to speak to him.

He got on the phone with his usual goofy-like voice and said, "Hellooo Deb!" That's all it took for the waterworks to turn on. He tried to make sense of what I was saying but it was hard to make out each of my words in between sobs. I calmed down long enough to tell him exactly where I was, and he told me he'd be right there. For the first time since the phone rang while I lay, curled up in my parents' bed, did I finally breathe a sigh of relief. Bobby would be here, and I would no longer be alone.

When my mom returned to the waiting room, she was wiping tears from her eyes, but I could tell she was on a mission. She explained that my dad was sleeping, and she had just sat and watched him. Now began the task of calling our grandparents, aunts, and uncles to break the news. Before any of those calls could be made, the first had to be to our house, where my thirteen-year-old brother sat there alone, waiting. Luckily, he hadn't been home when the call came in, so he missed all the commotion. He arrived home as the ambulance was pulling out of our driveway, so I'm not sure he really understood the brevity of the situation.

My mom reported that Michael was doing okay at home by himself. He was eating a TV dinner while watching his favorite show. She then, once again, disappeared into the phone booth, perched on the wooden half-stool that was attached, and began calling our relatives one by one. Sometimes sober, other times sobbing, she delivered the news. My eyes darted between my mom and the front door where Bobby would enter. As soon as I saw his blond hair, I jumped up and relaxed into his arms. He made me feel safe.

The only relatives that lived close to us were my mom's brother and his wife. They arrived about an hour later, at which point my mom ordered Bobby and me to go home to be with Michael. I protested because I wanted to stay as close to my dad as possible. He might need me. I know I needed him. My mom explained that I wouldn't be able to see him anyway and that if she learned anything new, she would call. I made her swear up and down that she would call with any information no matter how small. In the past, I liked to sometimes not know about the bad stuff but not this time. I devoured every piece of information I was given, trying to piece together the situation and figure out when I was going to get my father back. I didn't want this new version of him, I wanted the original. *I want that guy back NOW!*

Thankfully, my dad was released from ICU and sent down to a regular sick person floor a few days later. When I finally saw him, he was alert but different. He wasn't just physically different, but mentally something had shifted. It was hard to put my finger on it because it wasn't overly obvious. Something about his face looked different too. It reminded me of how in the movie *The Ten Commandments*, Moses goes up the mountain to see what the burning bush was all about, and he descends as a changed man. Of course, Moses' transformation was something of amazement and wonder. My father's transformation was more of a look of prematurely aged confusion.

I couldn't believe this was happening. It was like having a nightmare you try desperately to wake yourself from, but no matter how hard you try, you can't do it. The nightmare then just endlessly continues to play.

This was just proof that I had bad luck. I mean look at my life.

Strike 1: I was a fat girl in a thin family.

Strike 2: I was teased mercilessly, had my family hide food, so I wouldn't eat it, failed at countless diets, and was clearly flawed since I was still fat. Even though I *despised* being fat.

90

Strike 3: My father had an affair, and my parents separated. My Bat Mitzvah had been postponed and stuck in the calendar nine months later, on some random Friday night.

Strike 4: My father, my knight in shining armor, the only man who loved me more than anyone else, was now gone. At least the man I knew for the past seventeen years was gone forever.

Looking at the man lying in that hospital bed, I knew my life would never be the same.

On second thought… maybe I can!

Part II

Developing: The Transition

♥ 11 ♥

Dad or College?

"We cannot direct the wind, but we can adjust the sails."
—Dolly Parton

My dad spent the next two months in the hospital having different types of therapies to help with his cognitive and physical abilities. Bobby and I would go and visit him each day and bring him a veal parmigiana sandwich from Burger King—back then it was a limited time offering on their menu, and my father was obsessed with it.

All the employees at our local Burger King got to know us on a first name basis. Sometimes when I visited, my dad was chattier than others. Sometimes he seemed like his old self and other times he would be angry and sad, which was certainly understandable, considering his circumstances. My mom was also having an extremely tough time handling the situation. She had just turned thirty-nine years old and now had a disabled husband. She was still working and trying to figure out our financial situation, given that my father was no longer working, and it was starting to look like he would never again.

It was obvious that stress was eating away at her, but I had a chip on my shoulder. I felt that she wasn't being as kind, loving, and understanding as she should have been with my dad. I'm guessing my mom was struggling with the idea that she would now have to take care of the man who had cheated on her for the rest of his or her life, and that was not the life she had envisioned for herself. I couldn't read her mind, and since my main worry was my dad, it was my opinion that hers should be the same, too.

Someone needed to make sure that my dad felt loved and taken care of, and I was just the girl to do it. After all, this man was my hero. Although, having the affair did taint his hero status, I had made excuses for his behavior. The remainder of my summer was spent working and going to visit my dad in the hospital.

As the summer went on, my anxiety began to grow. At the end of August, Bobby and I were each going away to different colleges. I would be five hours from home, and Bobby and I would be three hours away from each other. Under normal circumstances, I would be petrified, but this situation with my dad added a whole new layer of worry and fear.

What if something happens to my dad while I'm gone? Who would take care of and love my father as much as me?

My insecurities were all bubbling up inside of me. *How would I ever be accepted in this new environment? People will take one look at me and snicker. No one would want to be friends with anyone who had a few extra pounds on her. Where would I change my clothes, so that no one would see? Would other people be able to see me naked in the shower?*

Pay Out

Barnes & Noble Booksellers #2140
319 Route 202/206
Bridgewater, NJ 08807
908-526-7425

STR:2140 REG:003 TRN:9664 CSHR:Megan C

Local Books   83.96

CASH   83.96-

Bookseller Signature

Manager Signature

Manager: Cox,Megan

061.01B   09/23/2023 03:26PM

STORE COPY

B.DALTON

BARNES&NOBLE
BOOKSELLERS

PAPER✳SOURCE

BOOKSTAR

B.DALTON   BOOKSTAR

PAPER✳SOURCE   BARNES&NOBLE
BOOKSELLERS

BOOKSTAR

B.DALTON

BARNES&NOBLE
BOOKSELLERS

BOOKSTAR

B.DALTON

PAPER✳SOURCE

B.DALTON   BOOKSTAR

BARNES&NOBLE
BOOKSELLERS

BOOKSTAR

B.DALTON

PAPER✳SOURCE   BARNES&NOBLE
BOOKSELLERS

BOOKSTAR

B.DALTON

PAPER✳SOURCE

BARNES&NOBLE
BOOKSELLERS

BOOKSTAR

B.DALTON

BARNES&NOBLE
BOOKSELLERS

PAPER✳SOURCE

BOOKSTAR

Pay Out

Barnes & Noble Booksellers #2198
319 Route 202/206
...ster, NJ 08807

STR:2198 REG:003 TRN:9664 CSHR:Megan C

Local Books $3.98
CASH $3.98

Bookseller Signature

Manager

Cox Megan

061,018   09/29/2023 03:...

STORE COPY

Unless you've tried it yourself, you have no idea how tricky it is to try and put your clothes on while covering yourself with a wet towel. No matter how hard you try, some part of your body gets exposed one way or another. Or you wind up putting on wet clothes because you try to cover up before you're dry. It's a lose-lose situation.

I was honestly torn. There was no doubt what I wanted to do. I wanted to stay home and go to college locally, so I could continue to care for my dad. However, there was a little voice in the back of my mind whispering to me that maybe college would turn out to be a good thing. If I didn't go, I would be missing out on this life altering experience. Someday I would look back and regret it. I didn't want that either.

In the end, it made no difference what I wanted, because my mother would not consider the option of having me stay home. She did not want me to miss out on my own life's opportunities because of my dad's health. She paid no attention to my pleas and arguments. The decision, her decision, was final.

Once I wrapped my head around the fact that I was going, I needed to figure out how I would possibly cope. This was going to be the first time that I was truly alone. No mom, dad, Michael, or Bobby to lean on. I hadn't even stepped foot into a store without another person, and now I was going to a school with 40,000 students. *How and why had I possibly decided that this was a good idea?* I felt so brave back in the spring when I made the decision to attend Penn State. Now, I hated myself for making this choice.

Saying goodbye to my dad was a crying fest for both of us. He had always been an emotional man, but the stroke had heightened that characteristic. Walking out of his room was one of the hardest things I had ever done. My heart ached terribly, and I wondered if I was doing the right thing.

The heartache continued when Bobby and I said goodbye to each other. I was leaving a day before him. The good news was that he was going to have his car with him, so we were already planning for him to come visit me. We figured it would be best to wait a few weeks to give us each a chance to settle in. A few weeks might as well have been a few years. He and I had been inseparable since the day we became a couple. We spent every minute of our free time together. I was not happy about what would become our new normal.

My mom and her friend were taking me to Penn State. As the three of us dragged all my belongings into my new home, all I could focus on were the other kids who all had their dads with them. They had their dads to do the heavy lifting and hook things up. My dad was lying in a hospital bed, trying to figure out if he would ever be able to use the limbs on the left side of his body again. I couldn't believe this was happening.

Saying goodbye to my mom was also very emotional for the both of us. My lips were still quivering long after they drove away and headed back home without me. They had dropped me off at some sort of prison and didn't plan on seeing me again until Thanksgiving. Talk about cruelty! *How does a parent do this to their child?*

My roommate was nice enough, except she had never met anyone who was Jewish before. She actually believed that

Jewish people had horns. *Wait, what?* I didn't even know where such a ridiculous idea came from. I was from New York where there were a lot of Jews. Even though my close friends weren't Jewish it made no difference. I guess she was as sheltered as I was. I had no idea that there were places in this country where there were no Jewish people. I guess we both learned something new.

I hated everything about school right from the start. Of course, I really wasn't giving it the old college try. My head and my heart were back home with my dad and three hours away with Bobby. I missed Bobby desperately, and I know he missed me too. The plan to wait several weeks to get acclimated flew right out the window. Bobby drove to see me before my classes even began. I'm sure my crying to him several times a day on the phone had something to do with it.

He was attending a satellite campus of Penn State and there was no housing. He rented an upstairs apartment in someone's home, and he had no telephone, so the only time we could speak to each other was when he called me from a payphone. I had been plopped down in the middle of Pennsylvania, with no way to get in touch with Bobby and just trying to survive each day, dreaming of the day that I could return home.

Seeing Bobby was the best possible medicine. When we were together, all was right with the world. My roommate wouldn't let him sleep on the floor in our room, so he would sleep in his car in the freezing cold. Occasionally, he would pick me up, and we would drive the three hours back to his apartment, which on the one hand was great, but it did present a different challenge. His landlord had told him and his mom that there were no dames allowed. Yes, he used the word "dames," which was way before my time.

I would have to sneak in when the landlord and his wife weren't home, or when we knew they were sleeping. Once inside, we both couldn't be walking around at the same time because then they would know that someone else was upstairs in the apartment with him. We also had to whisper very softly, which for me was particularly rough. I've been told a time or two that I speak very loudly. Regardless of whether we were at my place or his, it was stressful.

Meanwhile, back at home, my dad was getting ready to undergo an experimental surgery in Columbia Presbyterian Hospital in New York City. It was brain surgery to try and reconnect blood flow to the right side of his brain where he had suffered the stroke. The word "experimental," naturally, instilled fear in me. I needed to be there beforehand to see him and be there when he woke up—hopefully.

My mom, once again, told me no.

By this time, I should have known that my begging and pleading wouldn't work, but I had to try. I was desperate to be there. I asked Bobby to take me, but he convinced me that it was a bad idea. He didn't want either of us to have to see the angry look that would be on my mother's face when we walked into the hospital.

Thankfully, my dad survived the surgery, but it wound up being unsuccessful. After it was over, I finally convinced my mom to let me come home for a weekend, on my birthday, to see him.

Bobby drove three hours to pick me up and then another three hours to New York City. Once we arrived and parked, I couldn't get up to the room fast enough. Entering the hospital felt like I was stepping into a horror movie. The building was old with wide dark hallways and tall ceilings. I stepped off the elevator and made a left turn into an empty hallway. At the very end sat a man, hunched over in a wheelchair with white bandages wrapped around his entire head.

I was trembling as I walked toward the man, looking at the room numbers searching for my dad's room. As we approached the end of the hallway, my heart sank to the ground. The man in the wheelchair *was* my dad. The only word to describe how he looked was pathetic. A short three months ago, this handsome man was full of laughter and life, shooting hoops with Michael and me on the elementary school basketball court. Now, he sat looking like he had aged 1,000 years.

I tried to push back the tears and hide my terror as I greeted him. He lit up like a Christmas tree when he saw me. In that moment, I knew I was exactly where I was supposed to be. I spent most of the weekend at the hospital, and as I sat by his bedside, watching college football with him, and chatting, he asked me to come home permanently. I knew if he was in his right mind, he would never have asked, but now he couldn't hold back. He needed me! I was not going to let him down, but I needed to devise an escape plan from Penn State. If I came straight out and told my mom what he said, she would be mad at him and tell me that I was absolutely not coming home. So, I needed to figure out a different plan.

After a tearful goodbye, I assured my father that I would be back soon. I did what I said I wouldn't do, I asked my mom to let me come home. I didn't mention that my dad had asked because I needed to protect him, but I couldn't drive away without asking.

The answer was still an emphatic, "NO!"

Classes, grades, and school were no longer my priority. My sole focus became figuring out how to leave school. I knew there was only one person who could help me and that was my Aunt Judy. Aunt Judy, my father's sister, was and will always be my second mom. She was very different from my parents. She was loud, said a curse word or two, and had a relaxed attitude about life. My family was uptight. Uptight about everything and she was the opposite. This woman was *always* there for me. She and I spoke several times over the next couple of weeks. At first, she tried to convince me that school was the right place for me, but I wouldn't give in. She called my mom and spoke to her about the situation, but she didn't really get anywhere.

If Aunt Judy couldn't fix this, I was doomed. I was distraught and couldn't go to class. Instead, Bobby picked me up and brought me back to his apartment because I was inconsolable. I was so upset that I was unable to muffle the sound of my sobs. The couple downstairs knew there was a "dame" in Bobby's apartment. Bobby ran downstairs to explain while I continued to cry even harder. Now, I was going to be kicked out of here, and they would ask Bobby to move out since he hadn't stuck to their rule of "no dames allowed."

I waited anxiously for Bobby to reappear and relay the verdict. Surprisingly, they were understanding. Bobby told them about my dad and the situation. They allowed me to come into their kitchen and use their phone. I called Aunt Judy, and told her where I was, and that I was leaving regardless of what my mom had to say about it. She asked me to give her time. She would call my mom and try once more. I stood in the strangers' kitchen staring at the phone, willing it to ring. It seemed to take hours to hear the shrill sound of the phone. Aunt Judy had done it. I was finally going home!

On second thought… maybe I can!

♥ 12 ♥

Debbie the Caregiver was Born

"Be a rainbow in someone else's cloud." –Maya Angelou

After leaving Penn State at the age of eighteen, I returned home. I was splitting my time commuting to Hofstra University, working part time, and taking care of my dad. After a year or so, I decided I was ready for more. My dad had regained some ability in his left leg and was able to walk with a four-pronged cane. It was clear that he would never work again—he was permanently disabled.

My parents' marriage was falling apart but something inside of me longed for the true college experience. Commuting was fine, but I had no involvement or real ties to the local university I attended. It was clear to me that nothing I could do would change the outcome of my parents' marriage or my father's recovery. So, I decided to follow my gut and finish the last two years of school at The George Washington University in Washington, DC.

Bobby moved into my parents' house and became my dad's full-time caregiver. It was great because it gave me peace of mind. Bobby was great with my dad. He had recently lost his own father and he had a special connection with mine. Although, it was weird being away and having him more involved in my family's daily life than l was.

Going to GW was one of the best experiences and decisions of my life. I met wonderful people, interned for a congressman, and was really forced out of my comfort zone. I began to see how different life could be if I didn't allow fear to make all my decisions. During this time, I decided to forgo my dream of becoming an attorney. I was tired of going to school and was looking forward to graduating and starting my life with Bobby. Instead, I became an accounting major.

My parents had finally decided to divorce, and my mother went in search of places for my dad to live. He couldn't live on his own, and we couldn't afford to move him into most of the facilities in our area. The only place that met all the criteria was in New Jersey about an hour and a half away from home. Luckily, it was very close to my aunt and her family. They would visit him and bring him what he needed in between my visits.

Once the divorce was final, I was now completely in charge of my father's finances, health, and life, which was crazy since I was just learning how life worked myself at twenty-one-years-old. My poor dad was only forty-eight years old at the time, and he was living in a facility with eighty-year-olds. It was difficult for him to accept the divorce and his hopeless circumstances, so I spent a lot of time on the phone with him talking through his feelings. In hindsight, I should have gotten a psychology degree instead of a degree in accounting.

A few years after he moved to New Jersey, he found himself a girlfriend, Lucille. She was also a resident in the same facility but was only about ten years older than my dad, which was young compared to the other residents. There was something about her that I didn't like, but I wasn't the one in the relationship. She convinced my dad to get married and move out into an apartment of their own. I begged him not to do it. It had been so difficult for my mom to find a facility for him in the first place, and now he would be leaving it. I tried to convince him that they should share a unit at the facility, but there was no stopping him. He and Lucille moved out and rented a townhouse even further from where I lived.

We quickly learned that money was Lucille's motivator. My dad had received $25,000 when my mom sold our home, and she thought he was rich. This was the only money he had to his name—other than the monthly income he received from social security and disability insurance. He used that money to furnish the place, for the security deposit, and for rent.

A few months in, my dad called me saying he was concerned about his credit card bill. It turned out that Lucille had used my dad's credit card to buy anything and everything she desired from the Home Shopping Network. Once she realized that there was no more money, and that my dad was not rich—in fact he was downright poor and in debt thanks to her—her true colors were exposed.

She became verbally abusive to my dad and wouldn't help him. She would leave him in the shower, dripping wet, cold, and crying. I would get phone calls from him all the time asking for help. She was unhinged, and he and I were both afraid of what Lucille might do if he asked for a divorce, so we needed to devise a plan.

The first step was figuring out where he would live. At twenty-five years old, I had to go on a search and find a facility that was both nice and affordable. There was no internet back then, so it had to be done the old-fashioned way, which was by phone calls and yellow pages. I was living alone in a small condominium on Long Island and was thrilled when I found the perfect place only a mile from where I lived. Since the divorce, my dad and I had always lived in separate states so having him close would be great for both of us.

First, I met with the director, toured the facility, discussed finances, and devised a plan to move him to Long Island without Lucille finding out. Before moving him, I contacted a lawyer to discuss the situation and the divorce procedure. I never expected that I would be learning about divorce laws in the state of New Jersey at this stage in my life. Next, I needed to figure out the logistics.

Lucille had no idea that my dad was moving out and wanted a divorce. With the help of my cousin, Mindy, we devised a plan to "kidnap" my father. Lucille was going to visit her son for the day, who lived a couple of hours away. My brother rented a U-Haul and drove from Long Island to New Jersey with several friends who helped load the furniture we were taking from their apartment. The new place was only a studio, so we couldn't take too much.

Mindy supervised the move and left Lucille a "Dear John" note, explaining that my dad left and wanted to have no contact with her. The note did not leave a phone number or a forwarding address. Simultaneously, I took my dad to the local post office and bank to close out his account and leave a forwarding address for his mail. Life before the internet was much more complicated.

My dad and I then drove out to his new home, which he had never seen. The boys came with the van and set up his furniture. Lucille came home to find no living room furniture or bed. I wish there had been a camera in that apartment to see her reaction. She had tortured my dad. I had never met anyone who was so cunning and malicious and leaving her behind was a tremendous relief.

I had to take my dad back to New Jersey a couple of times to meet with the attorney. We never had any direct contact with Lucille, it was all done through the attorney. In the meantime, my friends were enjoying their carefree twenties. They were experimenting with their newfound independence. They were partying and traveling and doing what you should be doing at that age. They weren't dealing with their parents' illnesses or financial issues. That wasn't supposed to happen until you're middle aged. I was angry and jealous. *Why me?*

I learned all about the different types of "ologists," like cardiologist, hepatologist, and gastroenterologist. *Who knew there were so many different types of doctors?* I was also becoming an expert in the difference between social security disability, private disability, Medicare, and Medicaid. Each week, I would have to plan to get to a store, so I could buy my dad some snacks and visit with him. I was his only regular visitor, and he was always asking when I would be able to visit. I never wanted to disappoint him.

My holidays had to be planned around my dad. For all children of divorce, it's a challenge figuring out which holiday you spend with which parent, but for me it was even more complicated. I was my dad's lifeline, so if I didn't spend it with him, he would be alone, which was completely unacceptable in my book. All holidays with my dad would be spent in New Jersey with my aunt and cousins, and I was his only method of transportation.

My mom was very understanding about the situation, so thankfully it worked out. As time went on, my dad became a bit more ornery and more physically uncomfortable with the long ride, and his mood would often spiral into anger and frustration. Countless times I would have to leave after a short time because he was so miserable. I was infuriated because there was nothing I enjoyed more than spending time with my aunt and cousins. Dad had become a burden. I would need to make sure he was comfortable and had everything he wanted and needed *all* the time.

My resentment began to grow. I knew it wasn't his fault, but I wanted a life like my friends were experiencing. Becoming my father's caregiver had originally made me feel important and needed, however, after a couple of years that changed. Instead, I began to view myself as a victim and felt sorry for myself. *Why did I have this responsibility? This is NOT fair! Why am I so unlucky?* I had no choice but to accept the situation and deal with it, yet hardly a day went by that I didn't feel sorry for myself.

♥ 13 ♥

Life after College

"Some changes look negative on the surface, but you will soon realize that space is being created in your life for something to emerge." –Eckhart Tolle

I was excited to graduate from college and get on with my life. Bobby and I had recently gotten engaged, my dad had just moved into the facility in New Jersey, and I was officially an adult. The future was looking up—until it wasn't.

One by one, my world began to fall apart. I already had the responsibility of caring for my dad, who at that time was living in a different state. In addition, I would lose the love of my mother, my fiancé, and my best friend.

It had been a couple of years since Bobby and I lived in the same state so there seemed to be a bit of a transition period, at least that's what I thought. I noticed that he was acting strangely. He seemed busier than usual, but I figured that was because he had built a daily life that I had not been a part of. Many nights we couldn't see one another because he was working late or working on Saturdays. He was an electrician and he and his boss were the whole crew, and they had been working together for several years. During that time, I couldn't recall another circumstance when he had to work so much.

Sometimes, he would go out with his boss to a bar after work, which I thought was strange since his boss had a wife and kids. He was no longer making me a priority and it hurt. When we were together, he shared with me that he was working on this big job at a very large house. The owners had a live-in nanny to take care of their children. Neither of us had ever known someone who could afford a nanny, and Bobby seemed impressed, telling me stories about her. He seemed to be fascinated with her, and I didn't like it.

It took a couple of months, but Bobby finally came clean. He called off our engagement and told me he didn't feel the same about me anymore. I asked him if there was someone else, and he told me that he liked the nanny, but nothing had happened between them. I didn't believe him for one minute. Why would I?

My father had cheated on my mother and now it was happening to me. Every negative belief I had about myself moved to the forefront of my mind. *I'm unlovable. No one will ever find me attractive. No man will ever love me again.* These were exactly the reasons that I had stayed with Bobby in the first place. Deep down, I knew marrying him would be a mistake because we just weren't right for each other. I had agreed to marry him out of fear. I feared that no other man would ever love me, so I better say yes to the one who did—or at least the one who had at the time.

Bobby and I had been a couple for over five years. He was a part of my family. He was my partner and my safety net. We did everything together. With him, I was safe and protected. I was twenty-one years old and had never been to a shopping mall without him, my mother, or a friend. My legs grew weak, picturing my life without him.

I couldn't go down without a fight. After all, we had a lot of history together, which should count for something. I called his phone, but he didn't answer. I left messages crying, trying to create an excuse that would push him to come see me. It worked a couple times but when I cried, begged, and questioned him in person, the answer was still the same. He was done with me. It was over, and I would be alone for the rest of my life.

On top of my breakup, I also needed to move out of my house because of my mom's toxic, new boyfriend. Luckily, Joan was also ready to become independent. We rented a three-story-walk-up apartment together in a neighboring town. It was a dingy, dirty two-bedroom apartment in a not-so-nice neighborhood.

At the time, Joan was dating a guy who had a good personality and was friendly, but I didn't always like the way he treated her. Joan was crazy about him, and she had no time for me. When she was home, she was rarely without him.

My relationship with Joan started to suffer when I shared my concerns over her relationship with her boyfriend. It felt like I was losing her as well. I was completely miserable. No Bobby and now tension with Joan. Plus, I was on a liquid diet, which often left me "hangry" (hungry and angry), feeling deprived and sick, which certainly didn't help the situation.

I carried around this plastic jar and lid along with packets of powder, so I could have my "meals" anywhere. All I needed to do was fill the jar with water, add powder, shake strenuously, and drink. Drinking it was the hardest part because it tasted chalky and had a weird consistency. Each time I brought the jar to my lips, I would need to psych myself up to take a few big gulps. I had to get as much down as quickly as possible so I would avoid getting the full vile taste of the powder.

I got into a routine and the weight started flying off me, but I longed to eat. I wanted to chew and taste food but didn't want to cheat, so I turned to hard candy and gum. I figured neither were really food. Joan didn't need to worry about her weight. She was thin with drop dead gorgeous legs, just the opposite of me. She didn't have to think twice about what she was eating, so she bought chips, ice cream, and candy into the apartment. In those moments where I longed to eat, I would convince myself that just a little taste of Joan's food wouldn't hurt.

Drawing from my experience growing up with food hidden in the house, I employed the same strategy. I would try and just eat a little of the forbidden treat, so that Joan wouldn't notice. Once again, my plan backfired because once I started eating, I couldn't stop. Especially after a couple of months of eating nothing and only drinking vile shake after shake. I craved the good stuff.

Joan would come home looking to eat her chips and find only a handful left in the bag. She would be furious and yell at me. The tension grew so heavy between us, we both began avoiding seeing each other and when we were home at the same time it was uncomfortable. I berated myself for not being able to control my actions. I needed to figure out how to stay out of Joan's way. I was not one for confrontation or being chastised.

The only place I could go was home. Home to my childhood house, except I found out that that home no longer existed, thanks to my mother's new boyfriend, Dick. Let me just say the name fits the man. He was arrogant, conceited, and judgmental. *Why would my mother be with such a jerk?* I assumed that at least part of the attraction was his physical appearance. He was average looking to me, but he was tall, thin, and had silver and black hair. Physically he was the male version of my mother, so together, they might cause heads to turn. It made me sick.

Their relationship progressed quickly, and they were engaged. They had no reason to wait, so Dick officially moved in when I moved out. He came with a lot of new house rules that my mother allowed. My poor brother was a senior in high school, so he had to deal with Dick and his rules daily, but I didn't. However, it turns out I did need to comply with one of them. Dick's children visited on Tuesday and Sundays, so he felt it was appropriate for me to only visit on those days as well.

My mother insisted the rule did not apply to me. However, it was obvious when I showed up on a Monday night that Dick was not happy. I knew he didn't like me from the very beginning.

He thought he was "all that" and couldn't understand how anyone would allow themselves to be fat. He watched each and every morsel that went into my mouth to see if it was excessive. I quickly realized that I could barely eat whenever I was lucky enough to be invited over for a meal. I would either eat something before I arrived or have a snack waiting for me the minute, I got into my car to take the fifteen-minute drive back to my awful apartment.

Dick couldn't hide his disdain for me even when he tried. My mother would occasionally say something to him if he made a somewhat rude remark to me, but he would always say he didn't mean to be nasty. *What a liar!* I had never disliked anyone in my life as much as him.

One night when Joan was out, and I was in the apartment alone, Michael called me hysterically crying. He and Dick had gotten into a fight, and it had turned physical. He couldn't remember who had pushed who first, but eventually Michael ended up on the floor with my mother running in to break it up. Michael had jumped in his car to escape and sped over to talk to me in person. The anger bubbled up inside of me as my brother told me what had happened. It was one thing for Dick to mess with me, but it was another to mess with, let alone, physically hurt my brother in any way, shape, or form. Something had to be done.

As Michael sat across from me, relaying all the gory details of the altercation, I began devising a plan. I needed to figure out how to get my mother to wake up from whatever spell Dick had over her. She might like to be seen with him in public or enjoy dancing with him, but would that be worth sacrificing the loss of her children, not to mention herself? I had seen that Dick was an equal opportunity "judger." After their "honeymoon" phase ended, he would criticize my mother for not doing things around the house to his liking. He had an opinion on absolutely everything, including laundry, loading the dishwasher, and cooking.

I was shocked my mother laughed it off and didn't tell him to take a hike. My mother was not the kind of woman who would allow herself to be spoken to in that way. I couldn't understand why she allowed this type of behavior. If the tables were turned and Bobby had spoken to me like this, she would have insisted we break up. Suddenly, she was submissive. It all made no sense.

In just a few short months, life as I had known it had completely fallen apart. I had lost my mother, my fiancé, and my best friend. Losing one of them would have been bad enough, but all three at the same time was incredibly harsh.

Luckily, my cousin Mindy was my savior. She was living on the Upper East side of Manhattan in a great, one-bedroom apartment. It was the complete opposite of my current living situation. Almost every week, I would escape the reality of my world by spending the weekend with her. We would smoke pot and cigarettes and binge eat and watch movies all weekend long. Sometimes, we would venture out to Broadway shows, stores, or restaurants, but staying in her apartment was all I craved. It became a safe haven for me. It was a judgment-free zone. It was a place where I could smoke, eat, and forget about my life.

I hated when Saturday would quickly turn to Sunday. I would try to prolong my departure as long as possible. I would always want to watch just one more movie, so I didn't have to return to my apartment. On the ride home, I would pray that Joan wouldn't be there when I walked in. Each weekend would sustain me through the long, tortuous week I had ahead of me. Trying to deal with my new reality felt like I was trying to scale Mount Everest without first trying to climb a hill. I had no preparation or warning that I was to embark on such a climb.

I was the girl who didn't want to be seen. I was the girl who was afraid to speak up. I was the girl who was scared of her own shadow. I was the girl who never did anything alone. I would try to open up the old doors to work my way back into my mother's house, Bobby's arms, and Joan's friendship, but all attempts were fruitless. Just thinking about my situation would turn me into a trembling bundle of tears. I yearned for how my life used to be, but it was obvious this was not going to happen. Instead, I had to put one foot in front of the other and start climbing.

♥ 14 ♥

Joe

"You're worthy of being chosen, fought for, and loved. Remember that."
—Mark Groves

I'll never forget the day that my mother brought her new boyfriend, Joe, over to meet Michael and me. At that time, Michael and I were living together. We had rented an apartment in a beautiful two-family house his boss owned. I was twenty-four and Michael was only twenty, which was young to be living on your own, but after the Dick situation he had to leave. It worked out well for both of us.

My mother stopped by with Joe on their way to go dancing. At first glance, Joe was not the type of man either of us thought our mother would be attracted to. He was rough around the edges, and Michael and I both thought it was strange that he wore a huge lion head ring. It was so big you couldn't help but notice. They only stayed for a few minutes, so it was hard to form an opinion on anything other than first impressions, and neither of us were impressed.

My mother and Joe quickly became an item. We had been down this road before with Dick, so we were scared. The relationship between my mother, Michael, and I had improved dramatically once Dick was out of the picture, yet here my mother was once again bringing a new man onto the scene.

In the meantime, Michael lost his job and had to move back home while I moved once again, to a basement apartment in someone's home by myself. I hated everything about the place and never wanted to be there. Joe had already moved into our house and poor Michael was thrust back into the same situation he had been in with Dick. Michael was not happy. It seemed that Joe was not another "Dick," but the jury was still out. We didn't know him that well and things could change in an instant once someone gets comfortable enough to reveal who they truly are.

The first thing Michael noticed was that the refrigerator and pantry were stocked with food and not just any kind of food. There were cookies, ice cream, cake, and chips. Michael took one look at all the food, walked out the front door leaving my mother and Joe standing there wondering what had happened. He walked back in and told them he was checking the house number outside to make sure he had walked into the right house because never had our kitchen been packed with so many good things to eat.

I was welcomed at the house whenever I wanted to be there. Not only was I welcome, but Joe encouraged it. One night I had been over for dinner, and Joe had worked late.

He arrived home with his arms overflowing with containers from Baskin Robbins. He started to unpack the stash and the next thing we knew, there was a make your own sundae bar on our kitchen table. I looked at my mother to see if she was angry and was stunned to see a look of excitement on her face. It felt like we were at a party. There were four quarts of ice cream, all different flavors. Hot fudge, marshmallow, pineapple (my mother's favorite), and butterscotch sauce appeared along with sprinkles, whipped cream, and cherries.

My mouth hung open looking at all the delicious things on the table. I was unsure how I should proceed. I didn't want to be looked down upon for taking too much or putting on too many toppings, but after I saw how Joe made his own sundae, I knew I was safe. I never saw anyone eat like this, with such gusto and carefree abandonment. He was not judging anyone or expected anyone to judge him. This guy was starting to grow on me.

He had a wacky sense of humor and was fun to be around. He was unpredictable—you never knew what was going to come out of his mouth. Joe had been an excellent bowler, and he convinced my mother, Michael, and me to form a team and join a bowling league together. I would drive to their house every Tuesday night, and we would have dinner together before driving over to the bowling alley. We would bowl while laughing and having fun. It felt so easy and right. Each week Joe would tell us that if we threw a strike, he would treat us to ice cream after we were done.

The three of us would rise to the occasion. All of us wanted that ice cream treat. We were a pretty good team, often vying for first place, so we got to eat a lot of sundaes. I would always look forward to Tuesday because it was guaranteed to be a good time. I started to notice a change in my mom. She loosened up and was enjoying herself. There had been so many years where she had to hold it together and take care of our family that Joe gave her permission to not take herself so seriously.

Joe was healing our family. He reminded us how much we loved each other and enjoyed spending time together. My mother's house became a place where I wanted to be. It had become filled with laughter, love, and food. All the rules were gone. Joe had done away with them and if my mother would slip backwards, he would step in and gently tell her to back off.

He didn't just have a healthy impact on my mom, he did on me too. This man truly liked me. He didn't care if I was fat. He didn't care how much I ate. He didn't understand why I was so hard on myself. Joe encouraged me to loosen up, to stop always worrying about calories and my weight. He would tell me how beautiful I was inside and out. Joe was my mother's boyfriend, but he was truly my savior.

Now, of course, there were times when he drove me crazy. He could be extremely stubborn and pigheaded and wouldn't listen to anyone else's opinion when he was convinced he was right. However, just like all relationships, you learn to live with the good and the bad. At the time, my maternal grandmother was ill. She had a stroke and couldn't speak. She was living at her home in Florida with a live-in nurse. My mother would fly down once a month to check in on her and make sure she was happy and being taken care of properly.

Joe began to accompany my mother on these trips and became a huge source of comfort to not only my mother, but to my grandmother as well. He would help her physically and chat with her, even though Grandma's answers were unintelligible. It was obvious from my grandmother's face that she liked Joe too. But visiting her was stressful because after a while you didn't know what to say to her. It was hard having a conversation when one party couldn't really communicate.

One month, I decided to take the trip to Florida with them to visit her. Of course, there was a restaurant close to Grandma's that Joe loved. I had learned that everywhere Joe went, he knew of a good place to eat. It was a casual restaurant that had great hot dogs and ice cream. He had talked about how good it was and wanted to take me there, so I could see for myself. The three of us had our meals, and then the waitress brought out sundaes for each of us that were part of the lunch special. Joe took one look at the size of the dish and said it just wouldn't do. It was too small.

We started to dig in and quickly emptied our bowls. Joe asked me if I wanted another one. *Another one? Was he crazy?* I asked him what he meant, and he told me that he was going to order a second sundae and asked if I wanted one too. I couldn't wrap my head around the idea of ordering more. I had never even considered this as an option. I thought about what the waitress would think of us. *Would she tell everyone what gluttons we were?* I verbalized my concerns to Joe, and he told me I shouldn't care. He went on to tell me that I should only care what I think, and "to heck with everyone else." He reminded me that we would never even see this waitress again.

He asked again, "Do you want another?" I was terrified of being embarrassed, but also intrigued by the idea. I couldn't let this opportunity slip through my fingers, so I said yes. My mother passed because she needed to get over to my grandmothers to meet someone, so it was just Joe and me. The mother who would limit my food intake as a child was now gone and replaced by a woman who also had been enlightened by Joe. She didn't seem to care that I was going to have another sundae. I exchanged glances with her as each of our eyes opened wide, telling the other that this was nuts.

Joe and I ate our second sundaes while discussing my feelings of embarrassment. Joe explained that the only person's opinion I should care about was my own. We talked about how hard it was for me, and I begged him to tell me how to become carefree like he was. He shared that he had done what he was supposed to according to society's rules for most of his life. One day several years earlier, prior to meeting my mother, he had woken up and decided he wasn't happy and made the difficult decision to divorce his wife and upset his children. He had to do what was on his heart and in the process, he had hurt a lot of people. Since then, he had lived the life he wanted to and that included having more than one sundae. That was the day I officially fell in love with Joe.

Joe and I developed a special relationship. Several of his children, as well as his first wife and himself, had struggled with their weight. He didn't think it was a big deal and tried to teach me that I should feel the same. He became a mix between being a father figure and my friend. My dad was still alive, but our relationship had changed dramatically since the stroke. Joe wasn't taking his place but was an important addition. He was another man who loved me unconditionally. I wasn't embarrassed to put on a bathing suit in front of him or have him see me looking my worst.

He even became my fashion consultant and would come clothes shopping with me and my mother. He made the experience much more enjoyable for both of us and had a good eye for what was flattering, regardless of my size at the time. He tried to instill confidence in me and encouraged me to date. Placing a personal ad in the newspaper was popular at the time, and he insisted that I give it a try, regardless of how much I protested. He wrote my ad and put it in the newspaper. I would share with him all the responses that I received, and he would advise me on how to proceed.

Years later, he would become a grandfather to my boys who absolutely loved him and called him Papa Joe. He shared a love of sports, in particular baseball, which Sam (my oldest son) also loved. Joe would tell Sam stories about the players who were popular when he was a kid, and Sam would listen attentively. Joe would then offer both boys a sundae if they could answer his sports trivia questions. The boys, of course, would always be able to answer, and off we would go to get ice cream. He loved them as his own, just as he loved me.

For thirty years of my life, Joe played a significant role. He taught me so much even though he didn't have a college education. You didn't need a formal education to learn how to love yourself. You didn't need a formal education to learn to live life to the fullest. You didn't need a formal education to learn not to take yourself and life too seriously. He opened my eyes to the possibility of living a different life. A life that I actually enjoyed. A life where others' opinions weren't important. A life where I loved myself. Lessons that I'm still learning and practicing even though he's no longer with us.

♥ 15 ♥

Meeting Gary

"When two people fall in love, all they can think about is how to build the perfect world around them." —Anonymous

I was twenty-nine years old and still not married. Not only was I not married, but I wasn't even dating anyone. *How could this be?* When I was a little girl, I had this part of my life perfectly planned. I would get married when I was twenty-seven years old—I thought it was the perfect age to embark on a journey of creating a lifelong partnership with someone. I was then supposed to have my first child at the age of twenty-nine. Instead, I was still having crushes, just as I did when I was twelve years old. By twenty-nine, I was into the eighth year of pining away for my boss, Tony.

Meeting a man who would love me for me, plump body and all, had been a lifelong dream of mine. I longed for a partner to share and to create a life together. However, my dream was not to become a homemaker. I possessed no domestic abilities and had no interest in learning any. I did not cook and could barely clean. Having a partner was not going to preclude me from having a career as well as a life of my own. My mom had taught me the importance of being independent and not relying on anyone else. I did not want to care for a man in that way. I wanted an equal partnership.

I guess a girl is allowed to dream …

I had only one other short relationship since Bobby and I broke up eight years earlier. It was hard to meet people, and I was hoping Tony would eventually come to his senses, and we would be together—but no. At twenty-nine, it was hard to meet single men. Typically, you would meet someone at work, but clearly that wasn't working out for me. You might meet someone at a bar or a club, however, it wasn't really my scene, and, in that situation, you were approached only if you were pretty and thin. Clearly, that wasn't working for me either. A third option is being introduced to someone by a friend.

A few years earlier, my mother met a salesman through work, and they would chat every month when he came to discuss business with her. He was cute and single and looking to meet someone, so my mother gave him my number. He called me and we really hit it off. We talked on the phone for hours, day after day for several weeks. We had wonderful conversations and there was a lot of laughing and flirting. I really liked him, and I could tell that he felt the same about me. He was pushing me to meet in person, but I was scared. I was scared that when he saw me, he would change his mind. But if this was going to go anywhere, as I hoped it would, I had to do it.

We agreed to meet at a bar after work one night. The day before, my mother and Joe helped me pick out my outfit. I was going to stay in my "work clothes" because I felt more comfortable. I wore my favorite suit. It was my favorite because it made me look a bit thinner, so I felt more confident.

As I pulled into the parking lot of the bar, my heart was pounding so hard, I was convinced people inside would be able to hear the banging. I walked in, and he was already sitting at the bar. He was so cute, I couldn't believe it, but the minute he saw me he acted very differently than he had on the phone. I ordered a drink and after just a few minutes, he finished his drink, told me he needed to go, and ran out the door. He left me sitting there alone at the bar. It all happened so quickly; it was hard to understand what had just transpired.

I left the money for my drink on the bar, which I never drank, and ran to my car where I proceeded to cry so loudly that I was afraid people would come out of the bar to see what all the commotion was about. Deafening sobs escaped from the deepest, darkest part of me. I had to flee the scene of the crime as quickly as possible. I pulled out of the gravel parking lot trying to see the road through my sea of tears.

I talked to myself out loud while driving, berating myself for my weight and telling myself that I would never meet anyone. No man on earth wanted to marry, let alone date a fat woman. I couldn't bear the thought of going home to my empty apartment, so I drove straight to my mom's house. She and Joe had anxiously been waiting to hear how the date went and were shocked and upset when I burst through the door sobbing. They tried to convince me that the guy was obviously a jerk, and that I shouldn't let him get to me. Well, that was a lot easier said than done.

I decided if I was serious about finding a man, I needed to lose weight. Back to Weight Watchers I went, determined that this time would be different. And it was different. I was quite successful. Over the course of six or seven months, I lost fifty pounds and was feeling and looking amazing. My confidence level soared, and I was asked to become a Weight Watchers leader once I hit my goal weight, which was only ten pounds away. I was proud of myself.

I loved receiving compliments from everyone, including my clients. As part of my job as an accountant, I had small businesses that I visited monthly or quarterly. Some I looked forward to seeing on my calendar and others I didn't. I had my favorites and one of them was a plywood company. Their bookkeeper, Florence, was a woman who was a little older than my mother.

Each time I would visit, she and I would chat before diving into work. Florence had a daughter who was my age and was also having a difficult time meeting men. She didn't even have a weight problem, which made me feel better. I would share with her details of my crush on Tony. I would share the stories of the mixed messages he was sending me. She would offer me advice and tell me to move on just like the rest of my friends and family had been doing for years.

One month, we were chatting, and Florence mentioned that there was a salesman who worked there who she liked very much. She said that one day while she was chatting with him, she thought of me. Knowing both of us pretty well, she felt we would be a good match. We were having this conversation in her office with the door closed, so I couldn't see who she was talking about. She told me his name was Gary, and as she described what he looked like and where he sat, I didn't recall seeing him. Like two schoolgirls, we decided to leave her office and "casually" take a walk together to the filing room, so I could see what this guy looked like.

I did recall seeing him before but had assumed he was married. He looked married, whatever "married" looks like. He had a thick head of dark hair, a well-groomed beard, a mustache, and a pot belly. He was talking on the phone and laughing, leaning back in his chair with a foot up on the desk as we walked by. He reminded me of a young Santa Claus, and I had always been a huge Santa fan. I was definitely interested.

She made up some phony reason that she needed to see him, so he came into her office while I was sitting there, and she introduced us. We had a pleasant conversation, and he went back to work. As I was walking out of the office for the day, I stopped at Gary's desk to chat a bit more. He was easy to talk to, had beautiful eyes and a jolly smile (Ho! Ho! Ho!). I couldn't wait to come back again next month, so we could chat some more.

I made sure to wear my favorite outfit for my next visit. I had a lot of them now since I was losing weight. Gary was sitting at the front desk when I walked in, and we immediately started talking. The conversation was just so easy, pleasant, and comfortable. I could stand there and talk to him forever if I didn't have to actually work. We discussed the upcoming Super Bowl and how he was in charge of the office pool. He asked if I was interested in buying a box and of course I was. He explained that the numbers in your box were assigned randomly and would be picked on the Friday before the game.

He said he would call me that day to let me know my numbers, so I had them for Sunday. I gave him my number and was excited for Friday to come, so I could talk to him. I was planning what topic I could bring up when he called, so we had something else to talk about besides the Super Bowl pool. I was at a different client that Friday afternoon and the phone never rang. I didn't have his number, so I had to speak to him before he left at 5 p.m. At 4:15 p.m., I called the plywood company and asked to speak to him. He got on the phone and was his typical pleasant self. I asked him for my numbers, and he apologized for not calling. He had been busy and forgot.

Well, this wasn't a good sign. The next time I visited the client, Gary was sitting at the front desk and was very chatty with me. We were discussing golf. My mother and I had recently started taking golf lessons together. Of course, we both wanted to learn to play, but Joe had decided that the golf course would be the perfect place for me to meet a man. Anyhow, I was really starting to like this guy and hated the idea that I would need to wait an entire month to see him again. So, I did what any girl in pursuit would do, I devised a plan. I decided to show up at the plywood company one afternoon close to 5 p.m. under the guise that I needed to grab something from their files. Gary would have no idea if that were in fact true, and Florence was in on the plan, so it worked like a charm. I timed it perfectly so that I happened to be walking out of the building at the same time as Gary.

Our conversation flowed, and we wound up standing in the parking lot for over an hour. Gary offered to meet me at a driving range over the weekend to give me some pointers on my newly formed golf swing. I could barely contain my excitement when he suggested it, but I did a good job of playing it cool. On a beautiful Saturday afternoon in June, we had our first date at the driving range. Unfortunately, I wasn't sure if Gary was considering this a date, or it was just something to do on a Saturday.

Once we were done hitting, we stood in the parking lot talking for what felt like days. I kept waiting for him to suggest that we go to the diner or something, but he never said anything. As a last-ditch effort, I asked him what he was going to do after this, and he told me he had no plans. I told him that I was planning on going over to my mother and Joe's for dinner, and before I could think about what I was doing, I asked if he wanted to come too.

He said yes! *What have I done? This is going to be weird and awkward.* Luckily it wasn't. Gary had such a laid back, confident way about him where nothing seemed to get him flustered. My mother and Joe were shocked to see him walk through the door, but they ran with it and the next thing I knew the four of us were sitting out on the deck, enjoying the weather, eating, and playing cards. Boca, my mother's maltipoo was out there with us, and he started to run towards some geese that looked like they might attack him, and Gary jumped up to save him. I had found my knight in shining armor.

At the end of the night, we said goodbye, and each of us got into our cars. Gary said he had enjoyed himself but there was no indication that he had any interest in pursuing a relationship with me. We had no communication until my next regular monthly visit, which I had made sure to schedule in the afternoon since I only needed to be there for a few hours each month. Once again, we wound up in our favorite place, the parking lot. The conversation this time was about food and restaurants. He was talking about this great Italian restaurant and asked me if I would like to give it a try with him on Friday night.

Finally! We were going on an actual date. That Friday afternoon, I tried on every single outfit in my closet, looking for something that looked good and was the right mix of dressy and casual. I found something I felt good about and drove over to my mother and Joe's to get their approval. Gary picked me up there and off we went. We were there for several hours eating and enjoying each other's company. Things were going perfectly until he drove me back to my mom's. This time, instead of standing in the parking lot and talking, we were parked in Gary's car. I was waiting for him to make a move, but nothing ever happened, so I eventually said thank you and got into my own car.

I was perplexed. It seemed like he had fun and that he liked me but there had been no kiss and no asking for another date. *Was I reading this guy wrong?* It's not like I had a good track record with understanding men and their feelings. *Was Gary turning into another one of my crush obsessions?* My friends advised me to give it up because, clearly, he only liked me as a friend. The story of my life! As the days passed, and he didn't call me,

I was starting to think they were right. But in true Debbie fashion, I still believed I had a chance.

I had to wait weeks to see if my hunch was right. Back to the parking lot we retreated once again at 5 p.m. I was telling him that the dryer in my condominium had broken, and he offered to come take a look at it for me to see if he could fix it. I jumped at the offer and said in return that I would make him dinner.

The only problem was that I didn't cook. No, really, I don't know how to cook at all. I've always been a picky eater and never had any interest in learning the basics. Scrambled eggs, grilled cheese, and toast were the best I could do. Naturally, I went to my mother to ask how the heck I was going to pull this off without Gary knowing. This was going to be next to impossible, but I had gotten myself into this situation, so I had no choice.

I did as my mother instructed and bought some chicken, apricot sauce, rice, and string beans. The instructions I was given seemed fairly easy, and I was slightly confident I would be able to handle it. Gary arrived the following Saturday afternoon with his toolbox in hand. He retreated to my bathroom where my stackable washer and dryer resided. I heard a lot of banging while I started to cover the chicken in the apricot sauce. I went in to check on him after a while because he had been in there for a long time and never came out. Maybe he was on to me and was afraid he might leave with food poisoning.

Tools were strewn all over the bathroom floor along with drops of blood. I questioned him and told him to just leave it.

I certainly didn't want him to hurt himself. I did want my dryer fixed, but I could get someone else to do that. What I really wanted was him. He eventually did get it working, and we began to share a bottle of wine as dinner was cooking in the kitchen. I was really feeling good about the whole situation. The scene was picture-perfect, right out of a movie.

It was perfect until Gary asked if I smelled smoke. By this time, I had drank a glass of wine or two and had forgotten that I was cooking anything. He went into the kitchen and saw that the chicken was burning. He then looked at the rice and asked me if I had added the seasoning. *Seasoning?* I didn't even know I was supposed to do that. In a matter of minutes, we each learned quite a bit about one another. Gary surmised from the way I stood still, wearing a puzzled look on my face, that I had absolutely no idea what I was doing. Luckily for me, I learned that he did know his way around the kitchen. Furthermore, he was actually an accomplished cook.

Sitting down to eat the meal he had saved, I had to come clean and fess up. I told him I didn't cook, and I had no desire to learn. At this point, I might as well lay it on the line. He was amused by my confession. This guy was definitely for me, and luckily this incident seemed to seal the deal. From that day on, we were a couple.

Only a month later, Gary moved into my condo and six weeks later, we were engaged. There was no formal popping of the question but more of a discussion ending in the decision to get married. This decision came just a few days prior to my thirtieth birthday. It was truly a whirlwind, and my friends were concerned. They thought I was rushing into this relationship because I was turning thirty. I certainly understood why they felt that way, but I knew they were wrong.

This is going to sound cliché, but I just knew Gary was "the one." It was not a relationship built solely on passion, but on true love for one another. I could unapologetically be myself around him and not feel judged. I knew I was safe sharing the good, bad, and ugly parts of myself with him. It was the first and only time in my life that I was completely loved and accepted.

Soon after we were engaged, we had an argument that left me wondering whether I had made a rash decision. After all, Gary was the first and only person who fell in love with me since Bobby and I broke up. I called my mother, crying, and asked how I could know for sure I was making the right decision.

I assumed she would list different criteria to assess or that she would tell me not to rush into a marriage if I was not 100 percent sure. Well, I was wrong. Instead, she told me that she knew Gary was the one. She shared that she had known the first time she met him. We "just fit together like puzzle pieces in every way." I knew if my mother believed Gary was the one, then unequivocally, he was the one.

This was just the beginning of our happily ever after ...

On second thought… maybe I can!

♥ 16 ♥

My New Career

"If you don't go after what you want, you'll never have it. If you don't ask, the answer is always no. If you don't step forward, you're always in the same place." –Nora Roberts

Working as a CPA at a small accounting firm had its pros and cons, just like most jobs. For the most part, I enjoyed what I did, I was pretty good at it but just couldn't see myself doing it forever. I had begun working for a small accounting firm right out of college and never left. Tax season started in January and didn't end until April 15th. Those months were filled with twelve-to-thirteen-hour days, six or seven days a week. It was the perfect time of year to jet off to an island and escape the cold Northeast winters, but instead I had to watch my friends fly away to paradise while I punched away on my calculator.

The problem was twofold. The first was that I didn't really know what I wanted to do. I certainly wasn't interested in leaving and doing the same job somewhere else. The second problem was that I was scared. *What if I left and hated my new job?*

Or worse, what if I wasn't good at it? I was intimidated to look for a job in a big company. It would feel like being back in high school and since my weight was still an issue, I knew how that story would go. Working at a large company was not for me.

After eight years of doing the same thing, all by hand, we got our first computer. It became my responsibility to investigate, purchase, and install new software. I would then train everyone else in our office. Slowly, our clients also started to use computers, but many of them didn't use them for their accounting, only for their daily operations. It seemed to me there was an opportunity there for us.

I approached the two partners of my firm and shared my idea of creating a business where we would help our clients install and set up their books on accounting software. They liked it but needed to know more, so they sent me on my way to create a business plan. For the first time in years, I was excited about something. The business idea checked all the boxes for me. I was good at it, I enjoyed it, and I got to train others, which was my favorite part.

I could never seem to formulate a concrete business plan, and I put the idea on the back burner. Instead, I decided I should look for a job at an accounting software company. Simultaneously, my relationship with Gary was taking off, so my energy and attention were focused on him. My job no longer seemed so important.

As the months passed by, I found myself in a state of indecision. The business idea remained untouched, and the job search was put on the backburner. The summer breeze slowly faded away, and autumn arrived. Before we knew it, the year was ending, and Christmas was upon us. For the past decade, I had been celebrating the holidays with my dear friend Mary and her wonderful family. They had always welcomed me with open arms, treating me as one of their own. Mary's father, a seasoned insurance agent for a major carrier, had a deep love for his job. Mary had recently followed in his footsteps, becoming an agent herself and then moving to New Jersey to take a position as an agency manager. As we chatted about my job situation, Mary proposed a brilliant idea: why not become an insurance agent myself?

She explained the process, and how she might be able to make it happen for me, but we would have to move to New Jersey. I thought she was absolutely out of her mind. I had zero interest in selling insurance. I told her as much, and she said that Gary and I could do it together. Gary was a good salesman and enjoyed it, so he could do most of the selling, and I could handle the business aspect of the agency. It was intriguing but seemed far-fetched.

Mary and her dad were excellent salespeople themselves, because they spent the rest of the Christmas weekend telling us how perfect it would be. Gary and I agreed to move forward but knew there would be a lot of obstacles to overcome. The first was for the insurance company to agree to hire me. There could only be one agent, which would have to be me since Gary didn't meet some of their requirements.

I was concerned about the money we needed to do this, but Mary already had that all figured out. We could live with her for the first two years. The first two years, you were paid only half of the regular amount of commission. It was a probationary period, but once it was over, it would be smooth sailing. Next thing I knew, the process of becoming an agent had begun. I passed all the tests I was given. The next step was to find a location.

Mary explained that there was only one spot in New Jersey where I might be able to become an agent. It was in the town of Phillipsburg, which was right on the border of Easton, Pennsylvania. It was an area of New Jersey I was not familiar with, so one Saturday, Mary, Gary, and I took a ride and drove through the town. Phillipsburg looked like it hadn't yet come into the twenty-first century. It was an old steel town and looked nothing like Long Island.

But this was our only option. Take it or leave it. With Gary by my side, I had a lot more courage. Mary made it sound perfect and convinced us it would be a piece of cake. *When would I ever get an opportunity like this again? We would be our own bosses.* I figured the worst thing that could happen is that we failed, and we could move back home and go back to our current professions. My mom and brother no longer lived in Long Island, and I could move my dad to wherever I lived. We decided to take the plunge!

By Christmas the following year, we were set to open our agency on May 1, 1995. There was a lot to do prior to that date, so we would need to move in with Mary in January and leave our jobs before we began making money. We had to live off the money we had received as wedding gifts as well as use our credit cards. To earn some money, I would travel to Long Island on weekends and work there, especially since it was the busy tax season.

The agent who was currently in Phillipsburg had been there for forty years. His son, Rod, had worked for him and, in recent years, had been running the office. Rod was also becoming an agent. He would receive approximately two-thirds of his dad's business, and I would get the remainder. Our offices would only be a mile apart.

Rod's family was very well known in Phillipsburg's close-knit community. They were active community members and seemed to know everyone. Even though they knew the company rules, the family was not happy that someone, other than the son, would be opening an office in their town. Meeting all of them for the first time was quite intimidating since I was aware of how they felt, and I had no idea how we were going to pull this off. On the surface, most of them were friendly and kind, but I could still feel the undercurrent of dislike and annoyance—it made me very uncomfortable. We were outsiders, and if this was the Wild West, we would have been run out of town.

May 1, 1995 came and went without too much activity since no one really knew we were there. The customers had not yet received the letter in the mail, informing them that I was now their insurance agent. I assumed the phone would ring once they knew who to call, although I really hoped no one called because I was petrified I wouldn't be able to help them with whatever they might need.

Day two was the complete opposite. The letter from the insurance company had been delivered and the phones were ringing off the hook. Everyone on the other end of the receiver was screaming at me. They thought that I, a stranger, had rolled into town and stolen Rod's business. I tried to explain how the insurance company operates, how I would never steal anything from anyone. In the end, they really didn't care what I had to say. All they wanted was to be transferred back to Rod.

For our first two weeks in business, we received hundreds and hundreds of calls from angry customers demanding to be transferred. They hadn't even given us a chance. In just two weeks, I had lost over a third of my business. The company had to intervene and threaten Rod. He was supposed to be persuading people to stay with me by "selling" me to customers, but he hadn't been doing that. Instead, he was telling everyone that Gary and I were outsiders who had no idea what we were doing. He wasn't wrong, but that wasn't the point. The company replaced most of the customers who left by transferring different people from Rod over to me.

Each night on the hour drive back to Mary's, I would cry. The stress was becoming too much. On top of what felt like everyone hating us, we now needed to sell a certain number of insurance policies each month to make our quota and not be fired. We would stay in the office, calling people to try and set up appointments. It was typically 8-9 p.m. by the time we made it back to Mary's, where we were living in her tiny basement. When we arrived home, she would ask about our day and our sales numbers since she was our manager.

I hated it! I needed a break from the pressure. Gary and I were together 24/7 and we began fighting. As our first month came to a close, I had to prepare for the first of my four-weeklong training classes at our local headquarters. I would be attending this training with nineteen other new agents. Out of the twenty of us, I was the only one who had not worked for the company, prior to becoming an agent. Most of them were sons or daughters of retiring agents, just like Rod. Insurance was in their blood. They had been groomed for this.

We would all stay together in a hotel, and I would be rooming with another woman, whom I had never met before. I had never met *any* of them before, and my insecurities were playing on repeat like a movie in my mind. I felt like I absolutely could not do this. I cried and cried to Gary every day leading up to that first week. I was angry that I was the agent instead of Gary. He was so much more comfortable in his skin and being around strangers. I wanted to quit. I had had enough. We tried it and it didn't work out. This seemed like a good time to pack our bags and return home to our original safe and comfortable life.

Unfortunately, I was the only one who felt that way. It wasn't just about me. Mary had gone out on a limb to get me hired, and I couldn't or wouldn't do anything to make her look bad. I tried not to cry or tremble as I walked into the training room the first morning. Everyone was standing around chatting in different small groups, but since I didn't know anyone, I just took a seat. When the training was about to begin, the few people around me introduced themselves and were friendly. *Maybe this wouldn't be as bad as I thought.*

As with any large group, there were some people I liked and others I didn't. There were a couple of people who really took me under their wing. By the end of the week, I felt comfortable enough to ask them questions without fear of being judged for my lack of knowledge. They felt bad for me.

They said that this was hard for them, and they had been working in their father's offices for years. They couldn't even imagine what it was like for me.

Boy were they right. The first time someone came into my office and told me they needed to purchase homeowners' insurance, I thought about telling them I'd be right back, then running to my car and driving away. Instead, I excused myself and called Gary in. He was better at faking it than I was. After the customer left, Gary and I huddled together trying to figure out what we needed to do next to make sure the customer purchased the right thing.

As the months slowly went by, the stress didn't let up. We began to get an understanding of the tasks we needed to complete daily, which helped. However, the salary we were receiving didn't go very far. On several occasions, we had to call family members and ask to borrow money. In addition, meeting the monthly quotas was not easy. Each month, it would always come down to the wire, but somehow, we did it.

Working together turned out to be much more difficult than either of us had imagined. We were a team, yet my name was on the door and ultimately was the one who had to answer to the company. I was a nervous Nellie about everything, but Gary was much more laid back. He was also a procrastinator, and I wanted everything done yesterday. Our marriage began to suffer. Our business seeped into every aspect of our lives. If we weren't at the office, then we were talking about it with Mary. What else was there to talk about when Gary and I were alone? We were living in a bubble. In that first year, Gary quit three separate times, but it never stuck.

It felt like my world was crashing down around me. My marriage was a mess, my friendship with Mary was suffering, and I didn't know if we would be successful with the agency. I could lose my husband and my friend because I took a chance. It was a reminder of why it's better to play life safe. However, at this point, I was left with no other choice than to persevere.

After eighteen months of living with Mary, we moved out. It was time, and if it didn't happen, I would have lost one of my best friends. Financially it wasn't smart, but I didn't care. The credit card debt kept piling up, but, at the time, it was worth it. It was nice to have our own space again and to live closer to the office. It relieved some of the stress.

I could now see the finish line, which was May 1, 1997. Once that date passed, there would be no more mandatory quotas and double the pay. It felt like that day might never come. The days, weeks, and months went by so slowly, but the calendar finally progressed, and we made it.

I had been holding my breath for the past two years, and it was such a relief to let it out. I was proud of myself for not quitting. I was proud of myself for not giving into my fears. I was proud of myself that I was becoming a strong woman who could do hard things. I was proud to call myself an insurance agent for the best company in the business.

On second thought... maybe I can!

♥ 17 ♥

Infertility Struggle

"Strong women aren't simply born. They are made by the storms they walk through." —Anonymous

There was never a doubt in my mind that I would be a mother. I loved children and couldn't wait until it was my turn to have my own family. When Gary and I got married, we were thirty-six and thirty years old, respectively, so we didn't want to wait too long to get started. The first couple of years, we were going through a huge transition with our move and career change, so we decided to wait.

My brother and sister-in-law were married a few months after we were, and they had my niece two years later. They were a plane ride away, but we made it a point to visit as often as possible, so we could see our niece. Both of us loved her so very much that I could no longer wait to start our own family. The time would never be perfect, so we decided to ditch the birth control pills and try for a baby.

We tried and tried for about six months with no luck at all. I was upset, scared, and frustrated, so I made an appointment to chat with my gynecologist. He reassured me that this is not unusual. However, he suggested I take a medication called Clomid that would improve my chances—I was all over that! I'll swallow the whole bottle at one time if it would make me pregnant.

I was obsessed with reading everything I could about getting pregnant. I was taking my temperature before I got out of bed each morning—which was more difficult than it sounds when you have to pee so badly the minute you open your eyes! I would chart the temperatures to help me determine when I was ovulating. Once I calculated that it was time, Gary was alerted and had to be ready to go. After we were done, I would lay on the bed with my feet up on the wall, trying to help those little sperm to swim in the right direction. I would lay there wondering exactly how long I had to stay there as Gary popped up and went on with his day.

Several months of charting, taking Clomid, and elevating my feet, but I was still not pregnant. Each month when I got my period, I would be upset for days. When the cramps started coming on, I would try and convince myself the cramps might mean I was pregnant, but I was always wrong. My gynecologist suggested we try a form of artificial insemination in his office. I would still chart and take Clomid and when it was time, Gary would go into a room by himself and deliver his sample in a jar. The doctor would then take a turkey baster (not really, but that's what it felt like) and shoot the sperm inside of me. I would lay there for a little while and then would spend the next two weeks praying that I would not see blood.

We tried this for three more months until it became evident that it was time to bring in the heavy artillery. A friend of my cousin Mindy's just had twins via in vitro fertilization (IVF) and was clearly pleased with her outcome. Her doctor was about forty-five minutes away, but I didn't care. I wanted someone who I knew had been successful in the baby making business.

At first sight, Gary and I absolutely loved and trusted this doctor. He explained the process but told us that we were unable to begin now. Gary and I exchanged confused glances and asked why not. Before starting the process, we needed to address two important issues to maximize our chances of success. The first was that I needed to lose some weight. I was the heaviest I had ever been in my life after several years of some major league stress eating. I needed to lose over 100 pounds, but the doctor said losing just twenty or thirty pounds would really make a difference. My darn weight was once again the bane of my existence. The second was it was imperative to take care of my back pain before adding the physical stress of carrying a baby.

I had been dealing with a structural issue with my back, which had left me in excruciating pain for the past year. The pain had come out of nowhere and had been intensifying. It was difficult for me to walk for extended periods of time. Even a quick trip to the store had become too much for me to bear. Different doctors had different opinions on what type of surgery I needed, but they all concurred that I did need to have a spinal fusion, which was a major deal. The fertility doctor explained that becoming pregnant would only put more pressure on my spine and cause greater pain. In the end it made sense to have the surgery first.

Why did there always seem to be so many roadblocks? Nothing ever seems to come easily. I had no choice but to focus my attention on my weight and my back. I was like Dorothy in the Wizard of Oz who was told she must get the ruby slippers before receiving her prize of returning home. I was on my own quest to have a baby, so I got to work. Back I went to Weight Watchers for the umpteenth time. Fortunately, I lost thirty pounds prior to my surgery.

The spinal fusion surgery lasted for eleven hours, and I spent six rough days in the hospital. It was an excruciatingly painful experience, but I was a model patient. I did everything I was told by the doctor and physical therapists. I was in training, training to become a mother and nothing was going to stop me. We returned to the fertility doctor a few months after surgery, and he gave us the green light. I was ready. I was finally going to be a mom!

The doctor explained that before we discuss any specific fertility procedures, we, or should I say I, needed to have an array of tests. Gary needed to do stuff too, but the man got off easy. All he had to do was provide a sperm sample (poor baby!) and give blood. I was subjected to several painful tests. One was so incredibly painful, I cried through the entire procedure and begged them to stop. I couldn't believe that they did whatever they did to me while I was awake. It was literally inhumane.

I couldn't wait for the appointment when we would get our results. I figured we would hear that Gary's sperm count might be a little low and that, along with my weight, was the reason for our struggles. Boy was I wrong. Yes, Gary's sperm count was a little low but as the doctor explained to us in layman's terms, they were also a bit dumb. Instead of swimming upstream, they basically swam in circles. This problem the doctor said he could handle, but there was something else.

He took a breath and started explaining something about Inhibin-B. As he went on with his scientific explanation, in my mind, I was begging him to get to the point and tell us what my Inhibin-B deficiency means in terms of becoming pregnant. Finally, he told us that I basically had the eggs of a forty-two-year-old, even though I was only thirty-five years old. The bottom line was that I had rotten eggs. If I was to get pregnant, IVF would be the only way. He continued to explain the IVF process, which sounded terrifying.

Gary would have to give me daily injections of different medications. Some injections would be more difficult than others. Some would be subcutaneous, meaning it would be a relatively small needle that doesn't go too deep, like a diabetic's insulin injection. It could be given in either the thigh or stomach. Each day, I would need to come into the office for bloodwork and a vaginal ultrasound to see how the medication was working. The idea was to stimulate the growth of eggs so that when it was time to retrieve them, there would be enough there.

After the eggs were retrieved, Gary would contribute to the process by once again providing sperm (men get off so easily). The eggs and sperm are then put together to see how many eggs become fertilized. While this is happening in a petri dish in a laboratory, Gary would begin to give me a different medication, but this injection would be intramuscular, a bigger needle and different injection sites. This one sounded quite scary. *How the heck was Gary going to know how to do this correctly? What if he screws something up? What if he really hurts me?*

I was panic-stricken; however, I wasn't going to let my anxiety win. My desire to have a baby was far greater than my fears. *I will power through!* So, we began the process, and the shots weren't terrible. The hour and a half roundtrip drive to the doctor's office at six in the morning was a hassle but well worth it. Each day, in the afternoon, the nurse would call with the results of the blood test and let us know how much medicine should be injected that evening.

As the first week went on, it became clear that my body was not responding as they had hoped. I was not producing enough eggs, so it was time to bring in the big guns, the nurse explained. We had to add another medication, but this injection was intramuscular. Intramuscular injection now? I asked. Neither of us were mentally prepared for that one. Gary was afraid of hurting me and so was I! We were so terrified that we didn't speak for the hours leading up to the big moment.

The nurse told us to warm up the medicine first because it's thick and warming it will help to make it go in a bit easier. She also recommended icing the injection site (my butt) prior to receiving it. *Check and check.* I laid face down as Gary prepared to administer the injection. I tried not to tense up too much since I knew that would only make it more difficult and more painful, but it was hard not to do. One, two, three, *OW!!!!*

Gary continued giving me several shots a day, and we were each getting more comfortable with the procedure, except it seemed like I had bruises everywhere at different injection sites. The new medication did help to stimulate the growth of eggs, so thankfully, we were able to move on to the next step, which was the egg retrieval. I had been through so many painful tests and poking and prodding at this point, that I knew I could handle it. I kept reminding myself that I was strong. In the end, the retrieval was not something I wanted to do on a regular basis, but it was tolerable.

Now, we had to wait for five days and see what happened. The number of eggs retrieved were much less than a typical woman in her mid-thirties, and we had no idea of the quality. The quality would play a part in the number of eggs that would become fertilized. Each day we would receive a call giving us an update.

The first day we would find out how many fertilized eggs we had. Then, each subsequent day, we were told how many of those fertilized eggs were still alive and progressing appropriately. We would then return to the doctor after five days to have the blastocysts (that's what the fertilized eggs are called at this stage of development) put into my uterus. Then you hope, pray, and wait once again to learn if it all worked. Then hopefully you're pregnant.

My mood varied each of those five days after the retrieval, based on the information learned in the phone call I received. Of the eggs retrieved, only half of them were fertilized. Then each day, the number of potential blastocysts dropped like flies. The fewer the blastocysts, the lower the chances that this was going to work. In the meantime, Gary was still giving me those intramuscular injections to help prepare my body for becoming pregnant. Still, *OW!!!*

Four was the number. I had four blastocysts shot back up into my uterus to hopefully attach and grow into a little human. The waiting time from that moment until the pregnancy test, ten days later, was torture. With every little feeling in my belly, I wondered if that was the blastocysts attaching. I mean, I had no idea what it felt like to be pregnant. *Do you even feel when this happens? Maybe it was gas, not a baby.*

Endless days later, I returned to the doctor's office to have a blood test to see if I was pregnant. *This could be it.* Today was the day I had dreamed about my entire life. Today was going to be the day that I found out that I was going to be a mother. I tried to work that day but couldn't concentrate. The call came in at 2 p.m. I was at my office and my team member answered the phone. When I heard who it was, I called Gary into my office, so we could hear the news together. This was the moment I had been waiting for.

As the nurse said hello, I tried to read her tone but couldn't. She paused (felt like the longest pause ever), took a breath, and then said, "I'm so sorry." Instantly, the tears began to flow down my face as I asked her what would happen next. She told me to stop the injections and we made an appointment to come in and meet with the doctor the following week to discuss next steps.

I thanked her and fell into Gary's arms, sobbing uncontrollably as I hung up the phone. Here we were standing in my office with all this insurance stuff going on around us. I couldn't comprehend how any of that possibly mattered when my dreams were falling apart. There was no way that I could stay there a minute longer. I grabbed my purse and ran out the front door.

Gary followed me and made sure I was calm before I got in my car to take the twenty-minute drive home. All my friends and family were waiting to hear from me. They all knew today was the big day. Once I was home, I felt a bit calmer, until I called to relay the news to each of my parents. The hurt and pain violently shot through me over and over as I shared the news.

I then composed an email letting everyone else know the results. I was emotionally and physically exhausted and didn't have the energy to speak to anyone else over the phone. I tried to nap but sleep wouldn't come, so I turned on the TV. Of course, in the middle of the afternoon, all the commercials seemed to be geared towards moms. Lots of diaper and toy advertisements flashed in front of my eyes, bringing on more tears. *How could I possibly have any tears left? Is there an endless supply in our bodies?*

During the next week, I tried to turn my focus to my regular everyday life, but every time I saw a mom with a baby or a child, my mind went back to wondering if that would ever be me. It was excruciating to see all the kids in our neighborhood playing and laughing on their front lawns. There was only one other family who did not have children when we moved in, and they had their first child several months earlier. We were the only childless family in the neighborhood. Even my home was no longer a refuge.

A week later, when we sat down to meet with the doctor, I was still very teary. He said we could try again. The problem was most likely the quality of my eggs, but it was impossible to say for certain. I had to hope that I had a few more good eggs left in there, but there was no way to know for sure. There was no decision to be made, of course, we were trying again. Failure was NOT an option.

You have to wait a month before your next attempt. The process was the same the second time around, but it was easier because we knew exactly what to expect. Gary was comfortable with giving me the injections as well as mixing them as instructed. Each day, we would get a formula of what medicines to take, and he enjoyed playing mad scientist.

The medications were a bit different than last time, which gave me hope. I was sure that this would be the answer. It made sense that not everyone had it work the first time. Many days, while in the doctor's office, waiting to do bloodwork and ultrasound, I would get a chance to chat with other women. I heard all kinds of stories. I hung on every word, hoping to learn something that would make me believe that what I was going through was normal in the world of IVF and would ultimately lead to success.

When the day of the pregnancy test arrived the second time, Gary and I decided to take the day off and wait for the call together at home. I didn't need my team members and customers sitting there watching me fall apart if the pregnancy test was negative. I convinced myself that I had persevered through this process and my reward would be a positive result.

Negative again. I was not pregnant.

My legs were weak even though I was sitting, trying to digest the news. Immediately, my thoughts went to my usual place. *Why me? What had I done to deserve this? I am a good person. Why am I going through this?* I didn't know the answers to any of those questions. I was at a loss for words, but I knew what I would do. I was not going to give up. If I couldn't get pregnant with my own egg, I could get someone else to donate their eggs. Or we could adopt, but I wasn't quite ready for either of those alternatives just yet.

The doctor gave the green light to try again, so that's what we did. By now, Gary was so confident in his abilities mixing and administering the medications, that he was barely looking as he stuck me with the needle. I was a dart board, with lumps, bumps, and bruises everywhere. The whole process from bloodwork, ultrasounds, daily medication calls, and injections had become our new normal.

The third time there were four blastocysts to be transferred back into my body. This left me feeling cautiously optimistic for a minute or two as I tried to suppress thoughts of a possible failure. I was heading for a mental breakdown. This was a roller coaster ride that I never wanted to go on. In fact, I hate roller coasters, so I wouldn't want to go on one anyway. It was brutal.

Once again, we were home on the result day. I sat staring at the phone, trying to send the nurse a telepathic message to call. When it finally rang, I was startled and didn't quickly grab it like I had in the past. I wanted to enjoy the last few seconds of hope that I was feeling. I wasn't ready to plummet back down into the depths of despair.

I answered and the nurse had a different ring to her voice. She couldn't contain herself.

She blurted out, "Congratulations! You're pregnant!"

Did you hear me screaming back in the summer of 2000? My whole neighborhood certainly did. This time, tears of joy sprung from my eyes. I asked her about the next steps, and she explained that I would need to come in for blood work every day for a few days to make sure that the pregnancy was advancing appropriately.

Oh no! Something else to worry about, but that day I wasn't going there. I was going to enjoy the news I'd been waiting to hear my entire life. I was pregnant and going to be a mom! This time there was no reason to compose an email delivering the news to my friends and family. I wanted to tell each and every one of them myself. Joy, relief, and excitement simultaneously flooded my mind like I was living in a dream.

As I hit each early pregnancy milestone, I began to relax, enjoy, and savor each precious moment of the pregnancy experience. I was frightened when my fertility doctor released me into the care of my OBGYN, until I realized that now I was a "normal" pregnant woman with normal risks. I was the happiest pregnant woman on the face of the earth for the entire nine months. I relished each pain, kick, and feeling of discomfort. Until the actual birth, which turned out to be complicated due to my back issues. After twelve hours of excruciating back pain in labor with no medication, since the epidural didn't work due to my spinal fusion, I was taken to the operating room and given general anesthesia. I was sleeping when my baby was born.

In the end, none of that mattered because I received the best gift of all on March 21, 2001—Sam!

Once I had gotten over most of the adjustments that come with being a first-time parent, I was ready to add to our family. I didn't want Sam to be an only child. Even though my brother irritated me to death the first fourteen years of his life, I couldn't imagine my life without him. Having a sibling who knows exactly what you're talking about, who shares so many of the same memories (with a different perspective), and who is always there for you is such a blessing. I wanted that for Sam.

Back we went to the doctor a few months after Sam was born to learn what we needed to do to become a family of four. We had to repeat some of the same tests, and it turned out that my rotten eggs had become even more rotten than they were just fifteen months earlier when I had become pregnant with Sam. I knew the drill this time but having a baby at home, while going through the process, was much more difficult.

Once again, I did not get pregnant on our first attempt, so it was on to a second try. On round number two, something happened that hadn't happened the other four times. I did not have enough eggs to have the retrieval. I didn't even get up to bat. There was a minimum number of eggs needed for an attempt, and my body didn't produce enough.

I was completely devastated. At our doctor consultation, he agreed to give it just one more try, but after that, we would need to consider alternative options. I was mentally trying to prepare myself and consider my options but there was a small part of me that still held out hope that the third time would, once again, be a charm.

Each day I anticipated a call from the nurse, informing me that I hadn't made enough progress for the retrieval procedure. My sighs were as deep and loud as the big bad wolf when the nurse delivered the news that I was good to go. I made it to the retrieval with the absolute minimum number of eggs. Now, we had to see if any of them were fertilized.

A few did fertilize, however, one by one they didn't progress to the next stage. The morning of the transfer I wasn't sure if there would be any left. Each of the other times, I had three to four blastocysts to shoot on in there, but on the day before the transfer, I was down to only two. I had already been preparing for the inevitable failure by ordering a book on adoption and researching egg donors. I needed to have a backup plan in place.

Arriving at the doctor's office for the transfer, we learned only one blastocyst had survived, the other had not progressed. What could the odds be that I would get pregnant with just one? After all, I didn't get pregnant on three different occasions when I had three or four times that number.

Over the next ten days, I tried to focus on my alternative routes. When I got the call that I wasn't pregnant, I wanted to be ready to move on to plan number two. Having Sam was a lovely distraction. I spent my days being grateful for him and wondering how I was going to get him a sibling.

My wondering stopped the day the nurse called with my test result. One blastocyst was all I needed.

On December 31, 2002, Sam's brother, Ben arrived.

Our family was now complete.

On second thought... maybe I can!

♥ 18 ♥

My Annie

"Character cannot be developed in ease and quiet. Only through experience of trial and suffering can the soul be strengthened, ambition inspired, and success achieved."
—Helen Keller

Being the mother of two toddlers in my early forties was exhausting, but I knew I shouldn't complain. After all, being a mom had been a lifelong dream, and I had certainly gone through a lot to get here. I was busy juggling work and motherhood with no time to pay attention to my own needs. Joan and I had rekindled our friendship shortly after we moved out of our disgusting apartment back in 1986. She and I spoke daily. One afternoon, during our phone conversation, I was telling her how I was exhausted and just feeling a bit off. She asked about my symptoms and after I was done explaining them to her, there was a brief silence. She then told me that it sounded like I was pregnant.

Pregnant? Is she crazy? I just spent years and thousands and thousands of dollars to get pregnant. I had never been able to get pregnant on my own before, so it would be impossible for that to happen now at the age of forty-two. After we hung up, I couldn't get the thought out of my head. It didn't seem possible unless it was an immaculate conception since it had been over two months since Gary and I had done anything at night other than sleep.

My mind kept calculating dates and reviewing symptoms. I was torturing myself, but there was only one way to put this ridiculous idea to rest, so I bought a pregnancy test. The test was positive. *This was impossible. The test must be outdated and incorrect.* Good thing I bought two of them. When the second test confirmed the first, I told Gary the news. He was as shocked as I was when Joan first put the idea into my head. I knew the next call I had to make was to my fertility doctor, asking him how this was possible.

The doctor asked us to come in, so he could confirm the result himself. My at home tests had been correct, I was pregnant. According to the bloodwork, I was five weeks pregnant. *Five weeks? How is this possible when it has been over two months since Gary and I had been together?* I tried to push that thought out of my mind and listen to what else the doctor had to say. He explained when women are going through menopause, their hormone levels change and often they become more fertile. He went on to tell us that the chance of me actually having this baby was only five percent.

Well, those clearly weren't very good odds. I had begun to embrace this amazing gift I had received. I knew in my heart that this was my daughter. I absolutely loved being a "boy mom" but knew from experience that a mother-daughter relationship was much different. It was tougher in many ways, but in the end, it was very special. Since I was a little girl, I had known that I would name my daughter Jacqueline. I loved the formal name as well as the nickname Jackie. There was never a doubt in my mind as to my daughter's name, until now.

This baby that was growing inside me had to be named after my maternal grandmother. My Grandma Ann and I shared a special bond. It could have been because she often cared for Michael and me when we were younger. She would watch us when my mom was working, or we would stay with her and our grandfather when my parents went on vacation or just spent a late night out. I could tell her anything and knew I would never be judged. I told her all my inner secrets. She was safe, loving, fun, and full of life. She was never at a loss for words. She was a talker just like me. She understood my weight issues since she shared the same struggle in her life. However, she didn't care what dress size she wore. It wasn't important to her, and she tried to persuade me to do the same.

I was completely devastated when at the age of twelve, my grandparents announced that they would be moving to Florida. I didn't know how I would survive without her in my daily life. Over time, I got used to my new normal and had to be satisfied with phone calls and seeing her only a few times a year. Even so, Grandma remained my biggest cheerleader and someone who loved me unconditionally.

Each Tuesday, I would return to the doctor's office for a blood test and ultrasound. I would sit there, panicking, waiting for the doctor to deliver the news that my pregnancy was not progressing appropriately, however, that day never came. After a couple of weeks, we could hear Annie's (I just knew it was my girl) heartbeat. This was happening, but the tiny voice in my head, which was sometimes screaming, kept telling me this didn't make sense. The timing was off based on the only possible date of conception, but I guess miracles do happen. And I knew for sure that Annie was my miracle.

With each passing week, the impending feeling of dread and doom as Tuesday approached, began to subside. When Annie was eleven weeks old in my belly, the doctor delivered the news I longed to hear. Now, he was ninety-five percent certain that I would carry this baby full term and become a mom of three later that year. He was releasing me from his care and sending me over to my obstetrician.

A couple of weeks later, I took the forty-five-minute trip to see my doctor for the first time with baby number three. Gary had no need to accompany me since this was a first visit, almost like a baseline. There would be no new developments or ultrasounds, just a typical exam. When the doctor entered the room to start the exam, I excitedly told him all the details of everything that had transpired. He had already been through my journey with me and was thrilled to see me pregnant again. We were chatting as he was examining me until he asked me to be quiet while he put the stethoscope to his ear and pressed the other end of the cold metal onto my stomach.

He moved it around to different spots on my belly with an almost confused look. He then told me he wanted us to move down the hall to a different examination room, so he could do an ultrasound. I was a bit concerned but assumed it was because of my infertility history. I was excited. It was always thrilling to see a picture of the baby who was growing inside of me. After what seemed like an eternity, the doctor turned to me with a sad look.

"Deb, I'm so sorry. There is no heartbeat."

Maybe he's wrong. Maybe, we need to go to the hospital and use a more advanced ultrasound machine to detect the heartbeat. I didn't understand what he was telling me. The doctor kept talking, but I wasn't listening. I couldn't comprehend what was happening. This was my miracle baby who had already defied all odds. This was a gift sent to me from my grandmother. *This was my Annie.*

I was escorted out to the office area to use their phone to call Gary and tell him the news. The floodgates opened as soon as I heard Gary's voice on the other end of the phone. He could barely understand what I was telling him between the gut wrenching sobs that escaped from my mouth. When we hung up, I was escorted out into the waiting room as the doctor made the plans to schedule a D&C as soon as possible. I needed to be at the hospital at 9am the next morning to say goodbye to Annie.

It was all a blur, a nightmare I wanted so badly to end. After the procedure, I went straight to bed and wouldn't get out day after day. Gary had to stay home from work and take care of our toddlers, while continuously checking on me. Day turned into night and back to day again but none of it mattered. All that mattered was Annie. I never got to meet her. I never got to dress her in pink. I never got to comb her hair and put it in pigtails. I never got to teach her how important it was to become a strong, independent woman. I never got to experience the lifelong love and friendship I was sure we would share.

In my hours of despair, I reviewed everything that had happened since the moment of conception. *If in fact there had been something wrong with the pregnancy, as I initially suspected, why had I ever gotten pregnant? Why had there ever been a heartbeat? Why in a matter of weeks had I gone from the doctor saying I had a five percent chance to a ninety-five percent chance of having this baby?* I had been allowed to get my hopes up. I had formed a bond, a relationship with my baby, something that wouldn't have ever happened if the pregnancy had not progressed very early on.

I had to remind myself that I was lucky. I had two beautiful, healthy sons who needed me. I had to get out of bed. I had to pull myself together and stop crying. I had to be strong for my boys, they needed me. I somehow managed to get up, shower, and make my way downstairs to get back to living. The next several weeks I did what needed to be done, but rarely with a dry eye.

In just a few months, my world had been turned upside down. I had experienced nothing short of miraculous, only to have it taken away from me in the blink of an eye. However, in my heart, I will now always be a mom to not two but three children, Sam, Ben, and Annie.

♥ 19 ♥

Sam's Diagnosis

"You never know how much your parents loved you until you have a child to love." —Jennifer Hudson

I waited thirty-seven years, five months, and twelve days for my first son to be born, and Sam did not disappoint. He was the most beautiful, perfect baby I had ever seen. I know, I know, every mother says that, and we are all right. Each of our respective children are perfect. I was and am not the kind of mom that was good at setting boundaries. I was the mother who couldn't stand to let her baby cry.

I tried to do that "cry it out" thing at bedtime, and I'm proud to say I once made it for a whole thirty minutes before I caved. Gary used to joke that Sam would crawl back inside me if he could, because he wanted to spend most of his time attached to me, and quite frankly, I loved it. Sam made me feel needed and loved in a way that is indescribable—you just don't know until you become a parent yourself.

Sam and I signed up for Mommy and Me classes when he was just six months old. We quickly bonded with a mom and her nine-month-old daughter. We became fast friends and the four of us spent a lot of time together outside of our class. My friend Leslie's daughter seemed to be developmentally much further along than Sam, but she was three months older, and she was a girl. As we know, girls tend to develop and mature faster than boys. As Sam got a little older, I would pour some cereal on his stroller tray, but he would just stare at it. He didn't know what to do with it. I would have to pick up the little circles and feed them to him one by one. My little prince was very happy sitting back and allowing me to do the work. Leslie would joke that I'd still be feeding him when he was an adult. We would always get a good chuckle out of the situation each time I tried to show Sam how to do it himself, but he would make it clear that he liked it when I did it for him.

Sam was on the later side of all the developmental milestones but did achieve them in time. He had not yet said any words by the time we saw the pediatrician for his fifteen-month checkup. The doctor asked me if he followed directions. I didn't even understand what he was asking me. *I mean, was I asking a fifteen-month-old to take the garbage out?* I questioned the doctor, and he gave me an example like, "Sam, get the ball." I told him he often would tune me out when I asked him a question. I joked that it must be in the male gene since my husband often tuned me out as well. The doctor asked how I knew Sam could hear me.

I explained how much he enjoyed music and could watch the same videos repeatedly for hours. Sam would move his body to the sound of the music. I guess you could say he was dancing, but I had hoped that any child of mine would have a bit more rhythm (just kidding!). The pediatrician sent us for a hearing test just to be sure that all was okay. Once we cleared that hurdle, we were referred to our state's Early Intervention Program. This was a state funded program for children under the age of three who had developmental delays. Now, I was starting to really get concerned. *My perfect baby needed therapy?*

A lovely woman came to our home to evaluate Sam. She allowed me to stay in the room with them but had to ask me on numerous occasions not to interfere and say anything. If Sam didn't answer or respond appropriately, I was quick to make excuses or suggest to her that she try a different tactic. I wanted to ensure that Sam put his best foot forward. At the end of the evaluation, she told me that Sam qualified for physical, occupational, and speech therapy. I was shocked. At that point, I had only been concerned about his speech since he was almost eighteen months old and still hadn't uttered a single word. Developmentally, it was not unusual for children to say their first word somewhere between nine and twelve months. Sam was falling way behind, and it scared me to death.

A couple of months later, we went to see a developmental pediatrician to determine what, if any, disorder Sam had. I had been anticipating this appointment since we got it on our calendar a month earlier. I had made the mistake of going down the deep dark Google search hole. You know, where you type in a phrase like "diagnosis of an eighteen-month-old who doesn't speak" and you receive a plethora of diagnoses and more rabbit holes to travel down. After my research, I had him diagnosed and not diagnosed with as many disorders as there are Olympic events.

We met the doctor in an office where he had a few toys on the floor. He also kept a box of toys by his side that he took out when he was ready to observe how Sam reacted and played with them. Sam was leery. I think he must have sensed that this guy was there to label him in some way because he never warmed up to him the way he often did with others.

It was a grueling ninety minutes for all of us. I tried to offer opinions and recommendations to the doctor when asking Sam to comply with his instructions just as I had done with the evaluator from early intervention. I didn't want to see my child "fail" at anything, ever. Each time he was unable to properly follow a direction, I felt like someone had landed a punch in my gut. One punch after another landed with very few reprieves in between hits.

As the doctor was reviewing his notes in silence with his back to us, Gary and I waited, tingling all over with dread and anticipation. *Is this man going to tell us that our perfect son had some type of disorder? If so, would it be easily rectified?* Each breath seemed to cause a pounding sound in my ears while I stared at the doctor, silently begging him to turn around and issue his verdict.

His verdict was inconclusive. He explained how some of Sam's play, or lack thereof, was concerning, but his connection to us and eventually to the doctor was good. He reviewed with us several other points and in the end told us that Sam was young and that we would know more in about six months after he matured a bit and continued to receive his therapies through early intervention.

The last thing he told us was that in his report, he would diagnose Sam with Pervasive Developmental Disorder-Not Otherwise Specified (PDD-NOS). Another name more widely understood was Autistic Spectrum Disorder (ASD). To receive a diagnosis of Autism you had to have a specific number of qualities from Column A and Column B. If you didn't have that exact number but had some, then you received this catch all diagnosis.

The doctor explained that he was not saying that Sam necessarily had PDD-NOS (we'd know more at our next appointment), but by putting this diagnosis in his chart, our health insurance policy was more likely to provide more services and therapies for Sam. We thanked him because I was ready, willing, and able to accept any and all therapies that we could get.

My goal for the next six months was to make sure that Sam did not receive this PDD-NOS diagnosis. My friend Barbara had a child who had Autism, so she was extremely knowledgeable on the subject. She became my personal consultant. Barbara came over and ran through an array of her own tests to see if Sam would make eye contact and imitate her movements, similar to a simple form of Simon Says. Barbara seemed to be pleased with Sam's performance, but she and I both agreed that the more therapy the better.

In addition to the free services Sam received through the state program, I also took him to private speech and occupational therapy each week. Sam only had off on weekends, just like the rest of the world. He was a very busy toddler. In between therapy, I was trying to do things with him on my own, including our Mommy and Me gym classes as well as Mommy and Me music classes. I also started experimenting with sound therapy, where we would put headphones on Sam and play music and sounds that were meant to specifically stimulate different parts of his brain. He would have to keep the headphones on for two hours. In that time, there would be a therapist who would engage him in stimulating activities, and I would try to do the same when she was busy with other children.

I had the next doctor's appointment date in June 2003 etched in my mind. This was the day that could determine the course of Sam's life—the day when the doctor would tell us Sam's final diagnosis. I was doing everything in my power to make sure that he was not diagnosed on the Autism spectrum. I had already badgered all of Sam's therapists, asking for their thoughts on whether or not he had PDD-NOS. Some said no and others said they weren't sure. I tried to convince myself this meant that he would not be on the spectrum.

Gary and I barely spoke on the way to the doctor's appointment on that warm, sunny June day. As the appointment began, it seemed to be similar to the first time. The doctor gave Sam toys and gave him directions. He asked us some questions and as time went on, I was waiting for the judge to issue his verdict, but the moment never came. The doctor seemed to be wrapping up the appointment and hadn't told us anything. I boldly asked, "Does he have PDD-NOS?"

To which the doctor very matter-of-factly replied, "Oh, yes. Here's a brochure on Autism."

We silently walked out into the sunshine with Sam in Gary's arms. Once Gary had strapped Sam into his car seat, he turned to me and started crying. Standing in the parking lot beside our car, Gary and I embraced and sobbed. Our perfect, beautiful boy had a diagnosis, and we were scared.

I quickly went into mama-bear-beast-mode. My mission was to have Sam attending "regular" kindergarten and looking "typical." I stepped into an entire world that I never knew existed. They seemed to speak a language of their own. Welcome to the language of acronyms. I quickly got up to speed and learned the meaning of ABA, IEP, OT, PT, and CST just to name a few. I was extremely fortunate to have Barbara as my counselor. She explained why ABA (applied behavior analysis) was critical, but this type of therapy was not covered by insurance. You also couldn't just look up ABA therapists in the yellow pages like you could to find a speech therapist.

I was left alone on an island to figure out what Sam needed, where to find the therapists, and how to find the money to pay them. It was shocking to learn that there wasn't a handbook or a guide, like when you're diagnosed with anything else—like high cholesterol. They give you a pill and tell you to change your diet. *Why didn't this exist for kids on the spectrum?*

I put together my own team of therapists with Barbara's help and discovered a newer form of ABA that I preferred to the traditional style. In addition to therapy, Sam needed to be with his typically developing peers, but he was not able to handle the demands of a typical preschool. I found a school that would allow Sam to attend, along with one of his therapists. She would be there to help him understand the directions the teacher gave, help to facilitate appropriate playing with classmates, and be there to take him out of the classroom when his inevitable meltdowns would come.

When Sam wasn't in preschool, therapists would work with him at our house. I turned part of the master bedroom into a therapy room with all the supplies Sam's therapists needed. In a typical week, I was paying therapists between $25-$50 per hour (this was 2003 dollars) for approximately thirty hours a week on a regular basis, even though we couldn't afford it. I took out a home equity loan and began to accumulate large credit card balances. Each month, Sam's team of therapists would accompany Sam and me on a day-long training with our expert trainer, whose office was seventy miles away.

In addition to all of this, Sam still saw speech and occupational therapists weekly. I also experimented with other forms of therapy that required a great deal of time and money. Poor Sam barely had time to rest, although most of his therapies involved play.

As Sam made huge leaps and bounds, so did his peers, making it impossible to ever close the developmental gap between them. The Early Intervention Program ended at age three, and the public school district took over Sam's case. A couple of teachers from our public school came out to our house to meet and assess Sam. They explained to me how his day would be structured and what therapies he would receive once he turned three and attended the public school program.

Sam's day would no longer be in my control. Granted, there would be monetary savings, but I did not like the new program they wanted Sam to attend. Part of me thought they were the teachers, and they knew what was best for Sam, however, this other part of me that I hadn't even known existed, was awakened.

A year ago, I knew nothing, but it was only a year ago when I began to piece together my own team of therapists for Sam. It was only a year ago since I had decided on the type of ABA Sam would receive. It was only a year ago when I began to learn that I am Sam's voice. I am Sam's mother. I know best!

I made the decision that Sam would not attend the school's ABA program. They could not force me to agree to their services. I surprised myself with my voice and my confidence. The child study team (a group of school special education personnel) tried to convince me otherwise, but I stood my ground. Mama Bear had arrived and would not be messed with.

Of course, I knew that you "get more with honey than vinegar," so I was not disrespectful or nasty. I also learned to pick and choose my battles. I was becoming a master negotiator. Suddenly, other moms of children who had special needs were approaching me, asking for my advice. My best advice was to listen to their gut, it really does know best.

As with any organization, there were those who were just there to do their job and collect their paycheck and those who were there because they truly wanted to help kids. Each year as Sam aged, many of the players on his child study team changed, but it was easy to quickly decipher if they truly cared or were just doing their job.

When Sam was in first grade, and doing very well, the Director of Special Services at our school district asked to meet with me. She and I had disagreed on more than one occasion in the past four years but always managed to wind up coming to a place where we had mutual respect. I was shocked when she told me that she thought that I would make a wonderful member of the Board of Education. She explained that currently there were no other members of the board who had a child with special needs, and she felt as did I that it was important to have representation.

I played it cool as she was talking, but inside butterflies began flapping their wings. *Me, on the school board? What did that entail? Would I have to speak publicly?* I reminded myself that I did not enjoy being on public display or talking to more than a couple of people at a time. *What if I didn't know the right answer? What if I said something wrong and looked dumb?*

While all these thoughts were going through my brain, my mouth was asking her about the process. She explained that typically board members are elected by the public, but someone resigned in the middle of their term, so the procedure was different. I would need to contact the board president to say I was interested in the seat. At the next Board of Education meeting, which would be a public meeting—yes, I said public, like in front of other people—the board would interview all interested candidates. They would then decide on the spot. At the time, she hadn't heard of any other applicants.

No other candidates? That would work for me. It would seem I would be a lock for the spot, and maybe they wouldn't even need to interview me. I had many debates between me, myself, and I, and I won. I decided it was my responsibility to be the voice for all the Sam's out there. I can do this. I was ready.

I was ready until the day of the board meeting. I always seem to be brave when making the decision and then when the moment arrives, I'm thoroughly annoyed with myself for agreeing to put me in this uncomfortable nightmare of a situation in the first place. In addition, it turned out I wasn't the only candidate. There was another gentleman who had four children in the district (none of them with special needs) who was a great dad and overall, a good man. He was one of those guys who volunteered for everything. He was calm and easy going and professionally successful.

I was absolutely sick to my stomach as I opened the door to the middle school library where the meeting was held. There were approximately twenty people in the audience, including the Director of Special Services as well as my worthy opponent. The eight board members along with the Superintendent and Business Administrator sat at tables arranged like a horseshoe.

The meeting opened with the Pledge of Allegiance, and as I put my right hand over my heart, I had to press down firmly to stop my heart from ripping through my skin since it was pounding so hard. The board president explained the format of the interview and then the questions began. I wish I had the words to describe the fifteen or so minutes of questioning, but

I don't. Suffice to say, it was as close to an out of body experience that I ever had.

Somehow, words flowed from my lips in response to questions. When it wasn't my turn, I would listen to my opponent's answers with envy. He seemed to be so eloquent and knew just what to say. *Maybe someone had coached him. Maybe he's too polished.* My mind was racing all over the place. Once the questions ended, the board excused themselves and stepped out of the room to discuss our interview and make a decision.

This was a signal for everyone to stand and mingle. I did my best to smile and make small talk without letting anyone see the inner turmoil that had ensued. *Did I need to stay for the rest of the meeting and pretend I was interested? Would I look like a sore loser if I high tailed it out of there?* But I never learned the answer.

I became the next member of the Board of Education.

I had become the voice of not only Sam, but all the other parents and children of the school district. I was proud of myself and excited to make a difference. I had pushed myself far out of my comfort zone because not doing everything and anything I could to help my son was just not an option for me.

I had to remind myself of just how far I had come.

♥ 20 ♥

My 50th Birthday

"Friendship is the only cement that will ever hold the world together." — *Woodrow Wilson*

I love my birthday. I'm not talking about ordinary love, but over the top love. My age doesn't matter to me. I will be screaming from the rooftop (hopefully) well into my nineties. Unfortunately, so many of my birthdays had been overshadowed by all the trials and tribulations in my life. Often, Gary wouldn't rise to the occasion, and I wound up disappointed by it.

As I approached this milestone of turning fifty, I was a bit sad. Sad because my life was so difficult and complicated that I couldn't see how I could celebrate it in a big way, the way I wanted. I was also upset because my life didn't look like I thought it would at this age. I was having a pity party for myself, and I didn't need any others to celebrate with me.

Enter my posse, my three extraordinary friends, Mindy, Joan, and Mary. Now, I have been lucky enough to have gained two very special friends in the last twenty-five years, but my posse has been there for most of my life. First came Mindy because she's my cousin on my father's side. She's a year younger, so luckily, I only had to endure one year on this earth without her.

Mindy is a natural caregiver who approaches the job with creativity and thought. If she loves you, she's there for you in ways you didn't even know you needed. She prides herself on anticipating your every need, and she excels at it. She knows me better than most everyone else on the planet and is the only one who takes care of me, instead of me taking care of her. I think of her not as a cousin or friend, but as my sister. Her love and constant support are a true gift.

Joan expanded my posse back in 1976 when I met her in our seventh-grade social studies class. She was sitting in the row adjacent to mine, just a few desks in front of me. I would sit in class and admire her earth shoes. One day, I worked up the courage to talk to her and, as they say, the rest is history. A couple of my past stories highlighted our difficulties, but in almost fifty years the difficulties are just a blip in time. We have lived through marriages, divorces, kids, boyfriends, jobs, basically every aspect of our lives together. Our friendship has only strengthened over the years. We are there for each other regardless of day, time, or circumstance. If I call her and say, "I need you," she drops everything and comes running.

Mary rounds out my posse. I met her at GW when I was a junior and she was a freshman who graduated early and was really a high school senior. She was different than anyone I had ever met, but we had an instant connection. She came from a very rural, small town yet was the worldliest person I had ever met at the time. She wasn't like my other friends. She wasn't outgoing and gregarious, like Joan and Mindy. She never had a lot of close friends because she was an old soul and wasn't interested in the same things that her peers were. Not many teenagers loved Sinatra and WWII movies like Mary did. She and I seemed to be complete opposites, but as the saying goes, opposites attract.

My trio of friends all knew each other and had various interactions amongst themselves without me, but none of them talked to each other on a regular basis. In Mindy style, she insisted that I figure a way to go away on a short girl's trip to celebrate my fiftieth. I couldn't imagine being able to leave my family for an hour, let alone a few days. Gary's health was also on the decline, and the boys and their schedule were not easy to navigate, especially for Gary.

Mindy got Joan and Mary on board, and they decided that Bermuda was the perfect location. It was close, so we could go for just a couple of nights. Just the thought of the trip both excited and scared me, but after all I was turning fifty! Gary was nervous about it but wanted me to celebrate. It also got him off the hook. He and I had had many arguments in the past over his lack of forethought prior to my annual big day.

It was happening. I was really going away.

The celebration began at the airport the minute we were all together. We were talking and laughing so much, we barely came up for air. I couldn't wipe the smile off my face. Mindy, Joan, and I sat in the seats together and Mary was right across the aisle. The three of us made so much noise with our cackling laughs that I'm sure the entire plane couldn't wait to get off.

They probably developed a headache after being subjected to our loud voices. Mary on the other hand, was embarrassed by us but in a good-natured way, making it all quite funny.

We arrived at the hotel to find we had the perfect set up. We had two connecting rooms with balconies. Joan and I in one and Mindy and Mary in the other. As we unpacked, Joan started pulling out crowns, sashes, boas, confetti, and glasses in the shape of fifties. She began to decorate while Mindy and Mary were unpacking surprises of their own. I was so excited, so happy, and so carefree. It had been forty years since I had felt that way. I never wanted this to end.

They insisted I wear the fiftieth birthday pin and sash whenever we weren't in our bathing suits. We saved the boas, sashes, crowns, and other paraphernalia for nighttime. We swam in a cave where our voices and laughter were so loud that we were sure they would kick us off the island. We laughed so much that I thought I couldn't laugh any harder, but somehow, I always seemed to find there was more laughter inside.

I forgot how good it felt to laugh.

One night at dinner, I asked them if people used to know me for my laugh. It suddenly struck me, and I wasn't sure if it was true, or my mind was playing tricks on me. All three of them were shocked that I was even asking such a question. It was a characteristic of mine that made me stand out, mostly in a good way. I was always told that I could never get lost because wherever I was, you could always hear me laughing.

This trip had made me realize that for the past thirty years, I had lost my laugh. I had lost the core essence of who I was.

I had allowed my circumstances to rob me of myself. It was a sobering, yet eye opening realization. The first of many that I had on that trip. When we weren't laughing, we talked about each of our lives and our hopes and dreams. All my hopes and dreams revolved around my boys. I was a mom, first and foremost, and Sam and Ben occupied every fiber of my being.

However, Sam and Ben would eventually grow up and venture out on their own and then what? *What did I want for myself?* I hadn't ever thought about that question. It hit me like a ton of bricks. I forgot who I was as a person. I knew who I was as a mom, wife, caregiver, and boss, but not *me* as a woman.

The festivities of the weekend continued as we smoked the nicotine free e-cigarettes Mary brought while having a few cocktails on our balcony. I was dressed from head to toe in fiftieth birthday regalia and loving every single second. Before we had left for Bermuda, I thought I would be worried about Gary, Sam, and Ben the entire time. Shockingly, I rarely thought about them, once I had done my daily check in.

For the first time in my adult life, the only person I needed to think about was me. When the girls asked me what I wanted to do or where I wanted to eat, I didn't know how to answer. I wasn't used to my needs being the priority. It was fabulous!

I couldn't believe that I had agreed to only stay two nights. I wanted to stay in this cocoon with my posse forever. These women have literally changed my life in countless ways, but what they gave to me on that trip was truly priceless.

They gave me the gift of getting in touch with myself.

We chatted and laughed on the way home, reminiscing about all the special, fun moments we had shared over the last couple of days. Even Mary participated on the way back since we weren't quite as loud. None of us wanted the trip to end. It hadn't been special just for me. It was special for all of us.

It didn't take long to get right back into the swing of things once returning home. I stepped off that plane in Newark airport and the texts and calls started coming. Bermuda was quickly a distant memory, but the lessons I learned were about to cause a seismic shift in the course of my life.

I was now aware that my life had not been my own. I was not in the driver's seat. I had allowed others to steer for me, and I was just along for the ride. If I wanted to take a different route, guided by my own desires rather than the expectation of others, I needed to take control.

Awareness is what I had gained on that trip, and now it was my responsibility to put this knowledge into action.

Part III

Defining: The Present

♥ 21 ♥

Losing Weight

"You can't go back and change the beginning, but you can start where you are and change the ending." –C.S. Lewis

It had been eleven years since I lost a significant amount of weight. The weight had flown off while I was breastfeeding Ben in 2003. Once I was on a roll, I kept going because I did not want to be *that* mom who couldn't go down the slide with their child because they were too wide to fit, or if they could fit, their hips were wedged in, not allowing any sliding to take place. I lost weight once again by attending Weight Watchers meetings.

Over my lifetime, I've tried so many different weight loss programs that it's too many to count. Often, I would be looking for that quick fix. If I was going to suffer, I wanted the maximum benefit possible, meaning losing the most weight in record time. I have always wanted to be thin, and I've always wanted it yesterday. I've longed to be thin, not even thin, just average since the day I was born, but I had never achieved my goal, which really makes no sense.

After all, I knew how to lose weight, so why not just do it if I wanted it so darn badly?

I was up against having an internal battle with myself. I enjoyed food but was a picky eater, so it's not like I was constantly tempted by a variety of foods. If I could eat anything and not worry about my weight or health, I would be on a consistent diet of pizza, bagels, and ice cream.

If you're an alcoholic, you don't have to watch other people drink alcohol every minute of your life. Sure, you still need to deal with abstaining, however, you're not having someone else rub it under your nose reminding you that they can have something that you can't. I never could understand why I was being punished in this way. It was impossibly hard to watch others enjoy a meal that I wanted but couldn't have. I would look down at my sparse plate of bland food and throw myself a pity party. This would often lead to me coming home and searching for some type of treat, so I could rid myself of that feeling of deprivation.

I was able to go down the slide with Sam and Ben for a couple of years until the weight crept back on. Stress was my trigger, and I was experiencing a lot of it. At the time, my dad was beginning to need more attention due to health issues, Sam had received his diagnosis, and I was coordinating his therapies. In addition, I was trying to run my office while running both boys all over to different classes and activities. I didn't have the time or energy to pay attention to my diet. After a day of dealing with one stressful situation after the other, I wanted to plop myself down on the couch, throw a blanket over my legs, turn on the TV, and relax with a variety of snacks sitting beside me. This was my happy place, and I desperately needed that time to help me deal with my current reality.

Each moment that I sat there, snacking and watching TV, was simply heaven. Of course, I was creating another stressful situation because of my relaxation techniques. A month or two would pass, and my stressful day would begin the minute I tried to get dressed. I use the word "try" because I would have to try on several pairs of pants to find one that fit. Staring at the pile of clothes that no longer fit caused my blood pressure to immediately shoot through the roof. I had done it once again. I had lost a decent amount of weight, never gotten to my goal, and had gained it back along with a few more pounds than I had lost.

I was embarrassed and ashamed of myself. I had more motivation this time than all the other times I had tried to lose weight. Now I was a mom. I wanted to be able to play with my kids. I didn't want to embarrass them by being a fat mom. I wanted to live a long, healthy life, so I could be there for them for as long as possible (especially since I was thirty-nine years old when I had Ben). I wanted to set a good example for them by showing them how to eat well and exercise. I wanted to feel good in my own skin because I knew they needed a mom who was confident and strong.

All at once, my old, negative self-narratives overtook my thoughts. *If I can't be motivated by my kids, I'm clearly flawed. I have no willpower or discipline. I didn't even deserve to be a mom. I didn't deserve happiness. I'm literally a big, fat loser, and not the kind of loser I wanted to be (meaning loser of weight). I'm shocked that I even found someone to marry me. Of course, I had been at my thinnest weight when Gary and I first met … that explained how I managed to trap him.*

During this pity party, I decided that, since I was clearly destined to live my life this way, I might as well go all in and enjoy myself and eat whenever and whatever I pleased. Luckily, I came to my senses and knew gorging wasn't going to make me feel better. I decided to give weight loss another go and not be so hard on myself this time. I removed all expectations. I rejoined Weight Watchers and committed to going to the meetings and listening. That was all. I didn't even make a weight loss goal. This time I focused on the baby steps. So that's what I did. The next six months I faithfully attended Weight Watchers meetings every week and, in that time, only lost a couple of pounds. Losing a couple of pounds for someone who needed to lose 100 pounds was next to nothing, but I didn't gain anything, and that was a huge accomplishment.

My next step was to stick to the food plan fifty percent of the time. What I found was that it wasn't as hard as I thought it would be. In the past, I always had a goal that was time stamped. I needed to lose weight by the summer or by my birthday or a vacation. It was a lot of pressure and when I fell off the wagon, I fell way off and never hopped back on. I started to realize that I was never going to be perfect, but if I could remain consistent, that was okay.

The weight started coming off a bit faster, and I looked forward to my Saturday morning meetings. I loved the meeting leader. She was realistic, honest, and funny. I felt comfortable sharing in front of the group, which was new for me. I was comfortable sharing situations when I was proud, as well as decisions I had made that weren't the best. I find being part of a support group, where everyone shares a common struggle, to be incredibly freeing and therapeutic. It's so comfortable talking to others who just get it.

The next thing I knew I had lost forty pounds and was feeling great. I made the brave decision to give away the clothes I was shrinking out of, so they wouldn't be there to grow back into again. I couldn't wait to share my bold closet cleaning move with my leader and group the next Saturday, but when I walked through the door, there was a man there to lead the meeting. I figured he was just a sub, but he started the meeting by informing us that he would be our new leader. *Uh-oh.* I felt a bump in the road coming.

I tried. I really did. But it just wasn't the same. Every subsequent Saturday I had to convince myself to go to the meeting. My weight loss flattened out. I was in a loop of gaining two pounds one week, losing one pound the next. I managed to maintain what I had lost but made no further progress. One week after arriving, I was told that this meeting time and location would be closing. *Closing? How could they do that to all of us?* They gave us some other location options but none of them were convenient. I knew this had all been too good to be true. *Why the heck did I decide to give those clothes away? What a stupid grand gesture that had been!*

Once I calmed down, I decided that I wouldn't let this bump impede my progress. I drew strength, remembering all the other roadblocks I had encountered in my life, and how I somehow lived through them and had come out on the other side. I sat down with my calendar and a schedule of all the meeting locations and times and devised a plan. I would try a Sunday morning meeting in a location that was thirty minutes away, but I paired it with an exercise class that was halfway between my house and the meeting. I would drive thirty minutes and attend the 10 a.m. meeting and then drive fifteen minutes towards home and take the 11:30 a.m. dance aerobics class I enjoyed.

Turns out that the new meeting location was an actual Weight Watchers center versus the church where I used to attend meetings. They sold more products and overall had much more to offer. The meeting was packed and filled with energy and so was the leader. In all my years attending meetings, I had never been to a meeting like this before. It was filled with laughter and tears. People who seemed to know and care for one another. It felt like a family. I was impressed by the way the leader interacted with the members. This was the Weight Watchers home I had been searching for my entire life.

I was a turtle, different from the tortoise from the "Chicken Fat" song from my childhood. My weight loss was slow but steady and for the first time I didn't care how long it took to reach my goal. I had an epiphany. I was never going to be done with Weight Watchers or at least not going to be done with watching what I ate. All these years, I thought thin or average weight people were just lucky and us fatties were not. Turns out I was wrong. Of course, there is the exception to the rule, but I learned that I might have watched people eat a certain way at a party or out to dinner, but they didn't eat that way all the time. In fact, they most likely ate like that only once or twice a week. They had to pay attention to their diet too. It wasn't only me.

This had to be a way of life, for the rest of my life. I would certainly eat pizza, bagels, and ice cream again, but I wouldn't eat them every day. There was no end in sight and when I did indulge, or heaven forbid, binge, nothing bad would happen. It was up to me to put the binge behind me and get right back to my new lifestyle. Whenever my boys would comment on what I was eating, or not eating, they would say it wasn't on my diet. I would always correct them and tell them it's not a diet but a lifestyle. They found it very funny, but it was true.

The word "diet" had forever been stricken from my vocabulary. I hit the ninety-pound weight loss mark and received applause and pins and stars at my meeting. The leader asked me to be on a panel and answer member's questions about my journey. I was closing in on my goal and wasn't sure what that number should be. After all, I had never reached my goal in fifty-four years. I talked it over with my leader and my doctor and decided my goal would be to lose another ten pounds, making my total loss an even 100 pounds.

I was so close; I could taste it (not the best choice of words given the topic). The next few weeks I didn't make much progress. I gained a couple of pounds, but I knew that it could just as easily come off the following week. When I walked in to face the scale the next week, something felt off when I walked through the door. I scoured the room for the leader and didn't see her. Everyone seemed to be whispering instead of chatting loudly. I sat down and asked my friend what was going on and she told me that the leader was gone. Something scandalous had happened, and she was removed from this location. There would be different substitutes until a new leader was found. *Here we go again.* I couldn't believe it. I had found my Weight Watchers heaven and now it had been destroyed.

The scandal, which really wasn't such a big deal when the truth came out, changed the air in the room. Members who would come and contribute to the group were no longer attending on a regular basis. The new members who started were either not talkative or too talkative. The new leader was nice, but she wasn't like the original. My heaven had again been too good to last.

I hopped on the bandwagon of not attending every week. My schedule seemed to change, and other things took precedence. I sampled other meetings at locations closer to home, but nothing ever stuck. I started to gain back some of the weight. After the day I hit the ninety-pound mark, I never saw that number on the scale again. I watched the app on my phone count down but not in a good way. It showed my weight loss as eighty-seven pounds, then eighty-five pounds and eighty pounds. When the number hit seventy-six pounds, I started to panic. *This is not going to happen to me again.*

I went back to the basics. I committed to attending a meeting, weekly at a minimum. I was starting to get on a roll when the world shut down for COVID-19. All in person meetings were canceled, and like the rest of the world, Weight Watchers pivoted to virtual. It wasn't the same, but it was impossible to miss a meeting since there wasn't anywhere to go. I eventually found a meeting time and leader I enjoyed and was able to reel myself in and stop the backwards slide.

I once again found myself in the minority at the end of our COVID-19 lockdown. I hadn't gained weight; I had actually lost weight! I still wasn't back to the ninety-pound loss, but I was getting close. I had proven to myself that I can do this. It won't be easy. Sometimes it will be harder than others, but I just need to keep on trying. Quitting had been the problem. As they taught us in Weight Watchers, a slip doesn't need to become a slide.

We all slip. It's not something that only I do. Slipping is human. Sliding is my decision, and the only slide I'll be going down from now on is the one at the park.

On second thought... maybe I can!

♥ 22 ♥

Money

"Sometimes you don't realize your own strength until you come face to face with your greatest weakness." —Susan Gale

I've never been more scared and vulnerable as I am right now sharing this story. I'm typically an open book, feeling very comfortable to share my struggles with friends, family, and even strangers. However, there's one thing I've never really admitted to anyone in my entire life—at least not the whole, ugly, messy picture. I've revealed parts of this secret to a few, but never the entire truth.

It's time, but I'm scared. I know people will talk, and I'll be judged, but I'm sharing because the sole purpose of this book is to help *you*. Maybe you have a deep dark secret that you've kept to yourself, or it might just be so deep that you haven't even admitted it to yourself. I was that person. Anytime a thought crossed my mind regarding my secret, I would concentrate on pushing it down and force myself to think about something else because thinking about my secret was almost unbearable.

Here it goes …

I have lived most of my life in debt. Not just a little bit of debt, oh no. It started out that way and then it turned into hundreds of thousands of dollars. Seeing these numbers truly made me sick to my stomach. But let me start at the beginning.

It started when I was a child. Growing up, money was something we never had enough of. Now let me tell you that we lived a very comfortable middle-class life. We were not poor by any stretch of the imagination. We lived in a nice three-bedroom Cape Cod home in a suburban neighborhood. We always had what we needed but nothing particularly extravagant.

But to maintain that lifestyle, my parents had to accumulate debt. They had high credit card balances. I hated those Saturday afternoons when my dad would sit down at his desk and try to figure out how to "rob Peter to pay Paul." He would be angry and in a bad mood for the entire day. When his stress level was through the roof, we knew to stay away from him.

Michael and I learned to turn the lights off because electricity costs money and that "money doesn't grow on trees." My parents had a large circle of friends and many of them lived in nicer neighborhoods, drove luxury cars, and took great vacations. They wanted to have the same things their friends did, not that I can blame them. They had a bad case of keeping up with the Joneses.

Driving a Cadillac was very important to my dad. Cadillac's back then were the Tesla and Mercedes' of today. Every few years a new shiny Cadillac would show up in our driveway. It was my dad's prized possession. You could see his chest puff up with pride each time he got behind the wheel. Of course, as a kid I didn't understand that we really couldn't afford that Cadillac. I believe the stress of being overextended most likely played a part in my dad eventually having a stroke.

When I was a teenager, my parents decided that we needed to upgrade both our home and neighborhood. It was fun to go house shopping and see the inside of other people's homes, especially since they were bigger and nicer than ours. As we'd walk through, I would consider which bedroom I would want and picture myself hanging out and sleeping there.

All that dreaming was great, but I was a teenager. A teenager whose social life revolved around her existing neighborhood. *Couldn't my parents wait a few more years until I went off to college?* My mom loved a house that was thirty minutes away. She desperately wanted to move, and I desperately did not. I was completely traumatized.

After many long, drawn-out arguments, I prevailed, and we stayed in our town and only moved a few blocks away. It was a much more upscale neighborhood. I wasn't thrilled but couldn't complain since I was able to remain in the same school.

Once my father had the stroke, our money situation got even worse. We never had enough, but Michael and I were older and were working part time, so we made enough money to meet our own daily needs.

At home, money continued to be a huge source of stress. My mom had to deal with my dad's illness and the loss of most of his income. She walked around tense and distraught for several years.

I had learned that money equals stress. Period.

Fast forward to 1985. After graduating from college, I went out on my own and reality kicked in quickly. Suddenly, I was paying rent, a car payment, food bills, gas, and a college loan—just to name a few. I barely had anything left over to buy myself clothes or go out on the weekends. *Am I supposed to just sit home in sweatpants while everyone else was out enjoying themselves? That isn't fair.*

Hence, the start of my personal money journey. Right out of the gate, credit cards became my best friend and my worst enemy. If I wanted or needed something, I charged it. I would charge it and worry about the bill when it would arrive in the mail weeks later. After all, that's what my parents did, and they seemed to be doing okay.

It seemed like a good idea until the minimum payments of those cards continually increased as the outstanding balances grew. Before I knew it, I owed over $10,000 in credit card debt in addition to my car and student loans. The idea of saving money was a distant dream. I would tell myself that once I got a raise, things would be different.

Boy was I wrong.

Nothing was different because instead of using the extra money to pay down my debts, I just bought newer, nicer things. I moved apartments and each time I upgraded. I never gave much thought to my future or the debt that I was accumulating. I pushed all those thoughts aside and continued down the same path.

When Gary and I got engaged, I had to come clean. I was so embarrassed to tell him just how much debt I had piled up. At that point, I owned a one-bedroom condominium, drove a nice car, and had a mountain of debt. Gary was shocked. He had assumed that since I was a CPA, I would have had no debt and a nice nest egg.

I explained my various circumstances (really excuses, but I wasn't admitting that to myself), which had created my financial situation and confidently told him that together we would overcome it. He needed a few days to process the information, but luckily, he loved me, so he accepted it and married me—debt and all. Gary had been responsible with his money and lived a simple life in a tiny apartment. Other than a car loan, he had no debt but not much savings either.

This was just the beginning of my money story. The circumstances and amounts changed but my behavior never did. Once we were married, I was in charge of our money. Gary felt relieved not having to worry about it. It made him nervous, and I always tried to avoid making his anxiety worse. Otherwise, he would become hard to be around. I always had a story to tell myself and Gary. Keep in mind, I truly believed these stories. When I explained our financial situation to him, I wasn't lying, at least not for a long time. I never actually lied to him, but sometimes I didn't share the complete story.

There was a brief period in the late 90's when the stress of money was behind us. We had no debt and had excess funds to purchase things for our new house. The absence of a financial burden looming over our heads was exhilarating.

What was I to worry about if it wasn't money? Clearly, I felt the need to fix that.

First, I used the money to decorate our new house. Shortly after that, we moved on to all our fertility treatments and Sam's therapies, which were not covered by our insurance. I couldn't have predicted that we would need the money to start and help our family, however, I never changed any of our spending habits. Our flat, calm financial landscape grew into a pile, then a hill, a towering mountain, and then a mountain range of debt. I was silently suffocating.

I couldn't share the entire picture with Gary because when I did, it would send him over the edge. So I did what any good partner would do, and I dealt with it alone. Occasionally, the stress would overwhelm me, leading to an uncontrollable panic as I observed his excessive spending during grocery shopping. In moments of weakness, I would question his expenditures, which would cause him anxiety and prompt extreme reactions.

He would decide we couldn't spend any money, and he would slip into a depression for days. In these times, he was unpleasant to live with and barely spoke to us. Once I saw the correlation between money and his depression, I avoided sharing anything with him at all. *Why would I make him depressed when I didn't need to?* So I kept doing what I knew to do. Charging all our purchases and worrying about the bills when the time came.

I had become my parents.

As the years went on, I drained our large retirement savings, which we had been able to accumulate when times had been better. Once that was gone, I would not be able to pay our estimated income taxes (since I was self-employed, I had to make quarterly payments myself). Instead, I needed to use that money to pay my mortgage and buy food. I would delay worrying about the money I owed the IRS until April 15th of each year.

I would be able to pay a good amount and then would have to ask the IRS to pay the remainder in installments. This worked for a few years, but during that time my credit card balances continued to rise. Anytime I had to pay bills or look at notices from the IRS, I would do what I did best. I'd stuff it back down and not let the panic take over, but I was only fooling myself.

Deep down, I knew the situation was only getting worse. I knew that we no longer could afford our house. For a variety of reasons, our income had never been as high as it was the first couple of years when we first bought our house. Instead, it had slowly continued to decline year after year, but our tax bill was higher because I was taking our retirement money out to pay our bills. It was absolutely nuts, and only I knew what was happening.

As the years went on and the situation worsened my sense of shame and embarrassment intensified. I was constantly berating myself. *How could I, of all people, have allowed this to happen? I'm a numbers person. I'm a CPA and an insurance agent. I run my own small business. I should have known better.* I was a fraud. I might know the right things to do but I had never done them myself.

In February of 2020, Mindy and I attended Oprah's transformation tour. It was a full day of inspirational speakers, including Oprah and Michelle Obama. I had already begun to transform my life in other ways, but my money situation was quickly coming to a head. Nonetheless, I continued to resist confronting it.

Near the end of the day, Oprah told a personal story about a secret she had kept from herself. She asked the audience, "Is there any area of your life where you are not being honest with yourself?" Oprah explained how whatever that situation is, it will eventually explode like a volcano, and in the end, you'd be much better off owning up to it and finding a solution prior to the eruption. You might not like the solution that's necessary, but you'll be in charge.

I almost began to cry. As she spoke, I held back the tears, so Mindy didn't see and question why I was crying. Oprah's words penetrated me as sharply as a knife. *Oprah, you're right*, I thought to myself. As of today, I will no longer be an ostrich, sticking my head in the sand. It was time to take control.

On February 12, 2020, I resolved to change, marking a turning point in my life. This was only the beginning of my money transformation. I began to take stock of the situation. We were in so much debt in addition to what we owed the IRS, bankruptcy seemed to be the only option. Even though I was being honest with myself, I still wasn't telling Gary.

I went to see a bankruptcy attorney who explained that even if I declared bankruptcy, it would not take care of my IRS bill. At this point, the IRS wanted me to pay $8,875 per month, which was impossible. I had been dealing with the IRS for years, but our problem had grown too large, I needed an expert.

Google was the only resource I had when looking for help. No one else I knew needed to find an attorney to deal with the IRS for them. Cue increased feelings of shame and embarrassment. I was petrified that I would hire someone who didn't know what they were doing. This was a big, big deal and it was so scary taking a chance on an unknown person.

After reviewing my situation, they told me that they could help but it would most likely be a long, drawn-out process in its entirety, but I didn't care. It all sounded good to me. I gleefully turned my burden over to the attorney and breathed a sigh of relief. I still owed the money, but at least I wouldn't be afraid that someone would show up at my door telling me we needed to move out.

I then went on a mission to take other corrective action. I turned once again to a podcast for advice. In several episodes of a podcast I had been listening to, the host had talked about the importance of multiple streams of income. The concept made sense to me, but the execution seemed impossible. *This is for the wealthy, not someone like me.* I decided I would try and sell some items in my house that I no longer used or wanted. This would allow me to make a little extra money while also improving my mental health by cleaning out my cluttered home.

I was stunned to learn about all the websites that were out there to help regular people sell their stuff. I had absolutely no idea. I enlisted Joan to help me since she had previously sold some of her items. She took pictures and posted them for me. It hadn't taken me very long to find dozens and dozens of purses, jewelry, and other household items that were either brand new or barely used that I was thrilled to sell. Once I made the first sale, I was hooked. It became an exciting game, and I enjoyed selling things for any amount, regardless of how big or small.

I branched out and began posting on a website where I would need to ship the items sold instead of just leaving them on my porch for someone to pick up. It was certainly more labor intensive, but it broadened my audience and items started to sell quicker. I loved hearing the cha-ching sound on my phone when a sale had been made. I was constantly looking around the house for things to sell. It slowly became an obsession.

I launched into researching other ways to make additional money. I read books, articles, and listened to more podcasts. I explored various ways to make more income in my insurance agency and decided this is where I needed to start. I tweaked our sales processes and became focused on creating real change—something I hadn't been motivated to do in years.

There was no quick fix. Though rectifying the situation would require years of dedication, I was now confronting this challenge with unwavering determination.

I was on my way.

♥ 23 ♥

Becoming the Boss

"A comfort zone is a beautiful place, but nothing ever grows there." –
John Assaraf

I was scared out of my mind to leave my comfortable, yet unfulfilling job as a CPA to become an insurance agent. I hated the idea of becoming a salesperson. I was afraid. Afraid of talking to strangers. Afraid of not knowing what I was talking about. Afraid of being pushy. Afraid of not knowing how to run a successful business. Last, but not least, I was afraid of failure.

Without Gary by my side, I never would have agreed to stepping out of my comfort zone. He was just the opposite of me. He could talk to anyone about anything. He had an easy way about him, and people were naturally drawn to him. He had been selling for most of his life, granted it was plywood and building supplies, but selling is selling. He knew when and how to "push" someone and thrived on the challenge of making the sale. I assumed he would do the selling, and I would do the rest, whatever that would be.

211

The first few years as an insurance agent were an absolute nightmare. I soon realized that I needed to sell too. I viewed selling as teaching. My job wasn't to convince someone of anything. My job was to explain all the options and let the customer choose. This was something I was good at doing but didn't really enjoy. So anytime I could, I tried to push a customer over to Gary and let him handle it.

Regardless of your job, there's always some tasks that you don't enjoy doing or are scared to do. The thing that made my job different was that I had Gary who relieved me of ninety-five percent of those tasks. I had a list of non-preferred job duties.

I was uncomfortable speaking to people who were upset and angry. I had never had to deal with angry clients as an accountant, or at least, their anger wasn't directed at me. If someone was angry, I'd pass them on to Gary. Quite often, customers would be upset about the handling of a claim. Over time, Gary became our resident claims expert. He learned the ins and outs of both auto and fire claims. He had built relationships with claim representatives and managers within the company. Any claims problem went to him, and I was not interested in the details, unless I had to get involved as the agent since my name was the one on the door. Gary would walk me through what I needed to do in those situations.

Another thing I absolutely hated to do, was terminate employees. Over the years, we had some employees that we clearly needed to let go, and I struggled to muster the courage and have the necessary, uncomfortable conversation. I couldn't bear the thought of hurting someone even though I knew in the end it would be the best thing for both of us. Gary would be the one to break the news, while I was conveniently out of the office. *I was such a chicken!* Gary would save me, yet again, from facing my fears.

Gary and I each had our roles and responsibilities. We would occasionally bounce ideas and questions off one another but for the most part, we each did our own thing. We played to each other's strengths and weaknesses, and it was working. Occasionally, Gary would either lose his cool with a customer or not do what he had promised in a timely manner. I would then get a call from the customer complaining about Gary. *Awkward!*

Gary was a master procrastinator, and it was incredibly frustrating. I, on the other hand, would call you back in four minutes if I said I would get back to you in five. I prided myself on keeping my word and if I was unable to get a problem resolved in the time promised, I would always call the customer back with an update. My worst nightmare was having a customer say that I was unresponsive. This was a habit I could not tolerate from any of my team members, including Gary.

After a customer complaint, Gary and I would argue. I would be furious that he did or didn't do what he had promised, and he was angry because I hadn't defended him. After this happened a couple of times, I became a nag. If I was aware of a situation that he should be handling, I'd continually ask him about it. You can only imagine how that worked out. Each time I walked into his office, I would cringe because I could barely see him over the stacks and stacks of papers in front of him. Those piles scared me to death. They were his procrastination stacks. I would offer to go through them to see if I could help with anything, but he would never agree.

Eventually, I just had to let it go and accept this is who he was. Overall, he was a tremendous asset to the business. The complaints were far and few between and the happy customers far exceeded the few that had been unhappy. Gary wound up being the one that truly understood the most about the insurance business. His background helped him to understand the intricacies of calculating how much it would cost to replace a home and the parts needed to fix a car. Those things were way out of my comfort zone. I had no knowledge and no desire to learn any of it. Luckily, I didn't need to since I had Gary.

Working together also had its advantages. When the boys were young, we were able to stay home with them. I stayed home three days a week and Gary two. I was able to take Sam to whatever therapy I was dragging him to over the years. When my dad was dying, I was able to spend quality time with him during the day while Gary took care of things at the office. There were countless other times and situations where we had the flexibility and opportunity to do what we needed for our family without worrying about our jobs. We were incredibly fortunate.

We had developed a familiar rhythm that started to change when Gary was in his mid-fifties. I joked that he was going through male menopause because he became cranky and always seemed to have a new ailment. He had always suffered from social anxiety, which I never understood since he was such an outgoing person. But it seemed to intensify as he got older. We would have huge arguments when he wouldn't attend a holiday or party at my relatives' house. It had nothing to do with the people, who he loved, it just gave him anxiety.

Sometimes, he would be on his way to work (we drove separately) and would have to pull over to the side of the road to vomit. The first couple of times, I thought he had a virus, but as it continued, I feared it was related to his gastrointestinal issues. I would make appointments at doctors, but he would often cancel. He would either be too busy or had other more important things to do. He wasn't afraid of the doctors or what they would say, it just wasn't his priority. His art of procrastination at work, once again.

The diagnoses began to pile up: Crohn's disease, diabetes, depression, anxiety, and arthritis—just to name a few. He was taking so many pills and injections a day; I had no idea how he kept track. There were days when he would be in the parking lot at the office, and I'd be at my desk working when he would call. Once again, he wasn't feeling well and had to go home. As these calls became more frequent, I grew angry—angry because he wasn't taking care of himself properly. If he did see a doctor, he wouldn't follow through with the instructions he had been given. It was extremely frustrating as a partner, in both life and business, watching him hurt himself.

I began to feel like I had lost my partner. We no longer had date nights. We no longer celebrated holidays together (the boys and I went without him to my relatives' house). We no longer seemed to laugh as we used to. If I wanted to discuss anything serious, such as money, he would immediately become upset and would slip into a depressive episode. I could no longer share any of my worries or concerns with him.

He even stopped his trips to the grocery store, which had been his favorite thing to do. He had three or four different stores he liked to visit each week, which seemed crazy to me since the thought of visiting one a week made my skin crawl. He would explain how he could get different items at certain stores, and he enjoyed walking up and down the aisles and browsing. He also stopped barbecuing and barely cooked. The only thing that I had ever cooked for our family was toast, so we were in trouble.

The days he was able to get out of his car and venture into the office became unproductive. He would stay outside for most of the day, smoking cigarettes, or we would find him in a closet-sized room in the back, sleeping in a chair. His procrastination stacks of paper grew larger, and the number of complaints increased along with my anger and frustration. I made daily phone calls to my friends complaining about his actions and how my stress level was through the roof.

During one of these conversations, my friend Barbara asked, "Wouldn't it be easier to just tell him to stop working?" We discussed how the situation was already headed in that direction, so why prolong the inevitable? I was scared. Scared that now I was the one who would have to handle all that he had been responsible for. All the situations I was uncomfortable and felt incapable of handling. I had been holding on to the idea that he would somehow miraculously change back into the Gary I once knew, but rationally I knew that would never happen.

If I relieved him of the stress and pressure of working, hopefully he would be able to resume grocery shopping and cooking, which would be a tremendous win for the entire family. I had to rip the band aid off instead of slowly and painfully removing it. Barbara reminded me of the fact that we started this business knowing absolutely nothing, and over twenty years later we were still going strong. I had done this before, and I could do it again. I just hadn't wanted to, but it became clear that I had no other choice.

As I was still letting this idea marinate, one day Gary walked out of the office and told me he was done. I told him that I agreed it was best for him to be done too, but I needed to know what open tasks he had, so I could take care of them. I needed him to sit down with me and go through all the stacks of paper on his desk to see what was outstanding. I needed him to teach me a few things about parts of the business that he handled. This way I would feel more comfortable and prepared to face my new responsibilities without a partner.

It was too late. I had waited too long. He couldn't do any of it. He never could step foot in the office again. I tried to bring a stack of papers home to discuss them, but he couldn't, or rather, wouldn't. Somehow, I was going to have to figure out what he had promised to do for customers and take responsibility. I knew it would be impossible to figure it all out since his recordkeeping was subpar. Customers would call and be unhappy, and I had to be ready. It was bad enough that he was no longer going to work, but I couldn't understand how he could just leave me hanging like this.

With the help of my amazing team member Mary Jo, who had been with me for over twenty years, we sifted through the piles of paperwork and tried to figure out what needed to be done. If we were unsure, we called people explaining that Gary had to retire due to illness, and we wanted to make sure that all their needs had been taken care of. People were very understanding and asked to give Gary their regards and well wishes. It reminded me how popular Gary was with our customers and the person he used to be.

At home, nothing changed. He was unable to resume any household responsibilities. He spent his time sleeping and being very unproductive. We survived on take out and frozen dinners since I didn't know how to cook and had zero desire to learn. Grocery shopping was now my sole responsibility. My plate was already full and now this was one more thing I needed to worry about, as Gary sat home day and night.

Simultaneously, one of my team members, who was a tremendous asset, decided to stop working. She was kind enough to continue working longer than she wanted to support me through the transition of losing Gary. Now, I was down two experienced, licensed team members. Even if I found the perfect people to hire, it would still take quite a bit of time to get them trained, but I had no choice. I couldn't imagine a worse situation.

At times, the stress of it all was unbearable. I needed to let go of the resentment I was feeling towards Gary for putting me in this position in the first place. The resentment and anger were only hurting me. Over time, I was able to accept my situation and release those emotions. Mary Jo and I began to figure out what we each needed to learn to help us move forward. I hired a new team member, and we all began to create a new office environment. One that didn't include Gary's smiling face or his funny comments. It felt sad, lonely, and different for a while, but then we began to form our own unique bond as a team. A bond that no longer included Gary. I stepped into my new role of being the boss. I had technically always been the boss, but in reality, Gary and I had been a team. Now, all the responsibilities were on my shoulders and my shoulders alone.

Once again, I had no choice. My life circumstances had forced me to face my fears, and I had survived. I had done more than just survive, I thrived, teaching me that I was capable of anything. I could do hard things. I could do anything I set my mind to. I needed to give myself more credit.

On second thought… maybe I can!

♥ 24 ♥

Belly Dancing

"Twenty years from now you will be more disappointed by the things that you didn't do than by the ones you did do." —Mark Twain

It was New Year's Day, 2017 when I was invited to join a group of synagogue members for a walk along the Delaware River. I found myself walking and chatting with an acquaintance who I didn't know very well. Our conversation flowed easily, and we wound up talking about being insecure, which was intense and personal since we only had a superficial relationship.

As we shared our stories with each other, she mentioned that she took belly dancing classes. I was shocked. She did not look like a person who would ever do such a thing. I had no idea what I thought a belly dancer looked or acted like, but it wasn't this woman. I asked a million questions and told her that one of my biggest regrets was walking out of dance class at five years old and never going back.

She really encouraged and assured me it was a safe space, a judgment free zone. Luckily, there was a beginner class starting the following week. I left the walk energized and excited about the prospect of dancing, even though it was a type of dance I never, ever would have considered trying. I need encouragement to take the leap and someone to join me on this exciting new adventure.

I enlisted Lisa, a new friend of mine who I knew would be up for anything. We planned to meet weekly before class to have dinner. It would help to keep us both accountable. Neither of us had any idea what to expect as we stepped foot into the very small studio where the class took place.

There were only three other women besides us, which wasn't great because there would be nowhere to hide. The teacher was a woman in her sixties who had been belly dancing for over thirty years. She had long gray hair and wore glasses, also not the look I had pictured for a belly dancer. In addition, she had a much younger assistant, who was extremely overweight and wore an outfit that exposed her entire belly. Honestly, I was shocked. Here I was feeling self-conscious in yoga pants and a t-shirt, and she was confidently letting it all hang out.

This was going to be interesting ...

The class started with a warmup routine, which we learned would be the same every week. Much of it included movement to isolate each part of your body, which isn't so easy when you're a novice. I watched the assistant's body move in ways that I was unable to do. At first, when I looked at her, all I could see was her exposed girth, but in just a few minutes I forgot about that and watched how she moved her body.

Once we completed the warmup, it was on to learning a routine. The instructor explained that we would be learning one dance during our eight-week session. The steps contained the foundational elements that were necessary to become a belly dancer. I absolutely loved learning routines. Maybe it's because I'm a quick learner or because it just gives me a sense of accomplishment. It was a goal to work towards instead of learning random moves that didn't fit together.

It quickly became apparent that I was the fastest learner in the class and could move my body in the way we were instructed. Lisa, on the other hand, was not. She struggled with remembering the moves and executing them. The others in the class were somewhere in between, so the teacher had to slow the pace down, which I understood but didn't like. I was ready to keep going.

The assistant commented to the instructor on how quickly I learned and how good I was at isolating parts of my body. A brief back and forth conversation ensued between the two, regarding my abilities and promise. I'm not going to lie. It felt good to hear their comments. I was bursting with pride and excitement on the inside but couldn't really show it for fear of making the others feel bad.

I left the class feeling excited that I had followed through and attended class as well as the way I had excelled. Lisa said she enjoyed it as well, so we were off and running. We were going to become belly dancers. We stuck to our dinner and class schedule week after week. It was a lovely bonus that she and I got to know each other better and enjoyed each other's company. We would wind up talking so much that we would often have to dash out of the restaurant to make it to class on time.

Soon, our class started to feel uncomfortable for me because of the praise I was constantly receiving. It got to be a bit too much, and I felt the others were becoming resentful. Again, not going to lie, I loved it, but I felt it was a bit insensitive. Lisa would make comments that were supposed to be jokes, saying that the rest of them would never be as good as I was. I felt there was a tension forming that I didn't like.

Our eight weeks seemed to fly by, and it was time to sign up again. I was happy to hear that Lisa wanted to keep going, so we registered for another session. One night in March, the instructor announced that we would be performing our routine in May at the Hafla—a word they used, which basically meant a recital. I, simultaneously, was thrilled and petrified. My first question was what type of costume did we have to wear? I had been down this road only fifty years earlier, and I wanted this time to be different, but if she told us we had to bare our bellies, I was out.

She reassured us that the costume requirements would be basic and if we weren't comfortable exposing our midriff that would be just fine. *PHEW!* It looked like I was finally going to be in a recital. It was certainly a long time coming. Already, I was thinking about who I would ask to attend. After all, being in a dance recital was a big dream of mine. I used to tell my friends and family that I was going to take tap dance classes, and when I turned forty, I would perform at my own birthday celebration. Age forty and fifty had come and gone without tap class or a recital.

So this was my big chance!

We learned different subtleties of the dance, like your facial expressions and hand movements. Both were much more challenging for me, but not for Lisa. I had the moves in my feet and hips but lacked the drama of it all. Regardless, I was still in front, so everyone could follow me. In a sense, I was the lead, but it was a lot of pressure. I didn't like the idea of feeling responsible for everyone else's missteps because they were following my lead, but I didn't have much of a choice.

I began to practice at home in my kitchen. Gary and the boys would walk by and shake their heads and laugh at me, but in a fun way. They couldn't believe I was *actually* doing this.

As the recital date drew closer, we practiced how to dance and how to enter and exit the stage. I was instructed to make a slight movement with my head as the music began to signal to the other dancers it was time to start. We chatted about costumes and some of the other women had purchased outfits and brought them in. I was amazed how everyone was excited to wear traditional costumes, baring their bellies for all to see.

Out of the handful of us, my belly was probably one of the smallest, so why wouldn't I do it? I wished I could be that brave, but I was scared. It wasn't easy getting over a lifetime of shame and embarrassment because of my body. Although I was feeling the best I ever had about my body, I still wasn't confident enough to reveal my midsection. Lisa and I made a date to go costume shopping at a specific belly dancing store. Who knew such a thing even existed?

She and I were the only ones in the store, so the owner gave us her undivided attention. We explained what we each wanted and didn't want, so she had us try on a variety of items. I loved trying on all the different fancy costumes. I felt confident stepping out of the dressing room for the first time in my life. I was stunned when staring at my reflection in the mirror. Stunned to see just how good I looked. It was a lifelong dream come true and brought tears to my eyes.

I found a costume I loved that did not expose my belly, while Lisa's costume did. I was so impressed with the confidence that she had. She had an "apple" body type, so her stomach was proportionately large, while I'm a "pear," so my stomach is smaller. I found Lisa and my fellow dancers to be inspirational. They were going to wear outfits that they loved and felt good in, regardless of what anyone else thought. *I wish I knew their secret.*

I bought tickets for my friends and family. My boys were mortified by the idea, but I told them they had no choice. I wanted everyone there to witness my debut. I shopped for bracelets, earrings, and necklaces to complete the look of my outfit. The week of the performance, we met several times to have dress rehearsals, so we could perfect our dance. The teacher gave us instructions on what to bring that night, the time to arrive, and where we would change into our costumes.

In the months that I had been dancing, I had only met the women in my class. We were in the last class of the evening, so we never saw anyone else. When I walked into the room the night of the Hafla, which was not actually a room with a stage, but a fire hall with folding chairs placed in an arch around the room facing the front where we would perform, I was a bit disappointed. I had visions of stepping out onto a big stage with lights—not a dingy, dirty floor, but you've got to start somewhere, I guess.

Lisa and I went into the back room that was labeled as the dressing room and there was a flurry of activity going on. I was shocked at what I saw. Dozens of women, many large, half naked women, doing their hair and makeup. They were chatting and prancing around like no one was watching. I, on the other hand, was searching for a corner of the room where I could go to change. I wasn't one to prance around for all to see. Yet, I was energized by these women and the self-confidence they exuded.

We were the first to dance after the introductions since we were the beginner group. We lined up as we had been instructed, and as I peeked out into the room my heart began to pound, and my pulse quickened. I had done it to myself once again. I had talked myself into doing something and now that the moment had arrived, I was angry. Angry at myself for putting me in this situation. *What if I mess up? What if my family and friends thought this was ridiculous?* After all, we were beginners, so our routine was far from impressive.

For a split second, I considered getting out of the line and running out the back door, but that would be worse. The music started and that was our cue. My eyes searched for my group and once spotted, I looked around the rest of the room. It was funny how it felt like a lot more people were there once all those folding chairs were filled. Some people were smiling, and others had an uninterested look on their faces. I tried to focus on those who were smiling.

We got into our position on the "stage" and waited for the music to start, so I could give my cue. Once we were off and dancing, the music I had come to intimately know seemed to penetrate my mind, which allowed my body to move in the way it had been taught. In the beginning I was petrified, but once I settled into it, it wasn't so bad. As a matter of fact, I loved it. When we made our final curtsy to the audience and exited back into the dressing room, I couldn't help but want to stay out there.

Adrenaline was coursing through my veins, and I wanted to keep my dance party going, but my moment was over. I had caught the bug. I started thinking about how far my dancing skills would progress over the next year, allowing me to dance in more than one number. I found my friends and family and joined them to watch the rest of the show. They all told me how wonderful I was and how impressed they were with me. My friends knew how hard it was for me to put myself out there in this strange and unusual way, but I had done it, and nothing ever felt better!

We all felt a bit of a letdown when we returned to class the next time. We had all graduated to level two, and very quickly we realized we had a lot to learn. The warmup was harder than any moves we had done in the past. Lisa and I each seemed to take turns missing class for one reason or another. As the second year progressed, it was clear Lisa was not going to continue, and I needed to decide if I would do this on my own.

Most of my classmates were new to me, and we hadn't formed a relationship, so I did not feel warm and fuzzy dancing with them. At some point during the year, a new student joined us. She was so good that she advanced through the beginner's class quickly and was now joining us in level two. She became the teacher's pet instead of me, and I didn't like it. I found some of the moves quite challenging in level two but was still one of the better dancers.

As the second recital approached, I decided to be brave. After what I witnessed the year before, I knew that my bare belly would not be the one people would be staring at, so I was going to do it. I was going to bare my belly. This time, I had to go to the costume shop alone since Lisa had dropped out. It was no longer fun and exciting as it had been the previous year. This year I would dance in the opening group number as well as my level two dance routine, so I needed a second costume where I could just switch out a few pieces to make the costume change quickly and easily for the second dance.

Nothing felt the same as it had before. Lisa came to watch the performance instead of dancing. This year I didn't have as many of my friends and family in the audience either. Once had been enough for them, I guess. Back in the dressing room I really didn't have many people to chat with or to ask for help getting ready.

This year, I was in the opening group number with all the advanced dancers, which I loved. We hadn't practiced much together as a group, but somehow it all came together. I tried not to focus on the fact that the world could see my belly and instead focus on my moves. It was hard not to constantly hold my breath trying to suck the exposed flesh closer to my ribs. I couldn't wait to run back into the dressing room and cover myself, but I was still proud that I had faced my fear head on.

The performances went off without a hitch, and now I felt like I was practically a pro.

I moved up to level three, but I had to be honest with myself, I was no longer enjoying it as I once had. I think a big part of that was because of my classmates. The "teacher's pet" was still dancing and constantly being praised. I didn't seem to connect with any of them on a personal level, and even though I enjoyed the challenge of learning advanced skills, I didn't like the vibe in the room.

I began to come up with excuses each week as to why I couldn't attend class. I knew deep down that I was done, but I couldn't bring myself to really admit it and quit. I hated being a quitter. I questioned why I wasn't enjoying the company of my fellow dancers. I felt I would be letting myself down. I struggled with my decision, until Lisa made me realize that I had already done what I set out to do. I had taken a big risk by trying something new and had been brave enough to get on a stage and allow myself to be seen by others.

She was right. What I had done was a big deal and quitting didn't negate that fact. Maybe this particular class was not right for me at this particular time. This didn't mean that I would never go back to it, but if I did, it would be because I missed it and longed to belly dance again. If I didn't miss it, then clearly, I made the right decision.

I haven't danced since—but my dancing days are not over yet.

♥ 25 ♥

Becoming the President

"One of the greatest discoveries a man makes, one of his great surprises, is to find he can do what he was afraid he couldn't do." – *Henry Ford*

Can I tell you a secret? I'm afraid to say it out loud, but here goes nothing.

My dream is to be an inspirational speaker. Not just a small-town speaker, but a speaker on big stages, arenas, concert venues, and stadiums. I want to impact as many people as humanly possible by sharing my story and my message.

Phew! I can't believe I just put that out there into the universe. It's unbelievable to think that someone like me would be saying such a thing. You see, for most of my life, I've had no control of my life. Who was in control you ask? FEAR! You might be familiar with this emotion too. For my entire life, I allowed fear to rule the roost.

So I'm sure you're wondering how anyone who lives their life in fear would want to stand up on big stages and be seen and heard? Good question because it amazes me too.

Public speaking used to be on my top ten list of things I was most afraid of, right behind sharks (at least after *Jaws* came out) and the monsters lurking in my closet. As a matter of fact, for many years, it stopped me from taking on a volunteer position I had secretly dreamed of holding.

I had been very active in my Reform Synagogue for many, many years. I had been the treasurer for six years (not consecutively) and vice president (VP) for three. The succession plan was typically that the VP would become president, however, I would only agree to take the VP job if it was understood that I would not necessarily become president.

The last thing I wanted was to feel guilty about not doing what was expected of me. So why didn't I want to be president?

There were a few reasons why and all of them were ruled by my arch nemesis, FEAR.

What if I did a bad job? Maybe I wasn't cut out to be president. I would have to make a lot of decisions and judgment calls. It's one thing to make a bad decision, which only affects you, but it's another to do something that hurts someone else, let alone the entire organization. (I'm making my synagogue sound larger than it really is. We are a 110-family member congregation, but still.)

What if I couldn't effectively run a board meeting? We had a lot of smart board members who each had an opinion that they wanted to share. Often, the discussions would go round and round with each member vying for an opportunity to jump in there and be heard. *How would I possibly be able to control the conversation without hurting people's feelings?* Maybe the meetings would turn out to be counterproductive under my reign. It sounded like an extremely uncomfortable and impossible situation for someone like me to handle.

I would have to run our annual, congregational meeting. This is a year in review meeting to update the congregation on the current situation. In the past, the meetings were not very well attended, unless there was a controversial issue on the agenda. *What if there wound up being a matter that drove people to show up when I was president?* Chances were, they would be upset and would want answers. *What if I didn't know the answers? What if I had no idea what to say and I said something stupid?* I'm not someone who is good under pressure, so definitely not the right person for the job.

Last, but not least, the thing that terrified me the most about being president was the responsibility of addressing the congregation from the pulpit during the High Holy Days. It is the president's job on Rosh Hashanah and Yom Kippur (ten days apart) to give a speech during services asking the congregation for financial support. Attendance for these two days was not questionable. Oh no, these days are the best attended days of the year. There could be approximately 150 people in the synagogue. That's 149 more than I was comfortable talking to at a time. This responsibility sealed the deal for me. I would never be president!

It was February of 2018 when the call came in. The call I had been dreading. The call I had thought about repeatedly in my mind. The call asking if I would become president when our new fiscal year began on July 1, 2018.

Based on the reasons above, my answer should have been an emphatic "thanks, but no thanks" but that's not what I said. Instead, I said, "I would be honored."

Wait. What??? You read that right. I was as shocked as you are.

Two different thoughts had been on repeat in my mind for months while considering this decision. The first was that my dad had always wanted to be president of our congregation and a year prior to him taking on that title, he had the stroke. My dad had passed away in 2011, and I felt that I would somehow be living out his dream for him. How could I say no?

The other loop playing in my head was that I was fifty-five years old, and I was still allowing fear to control me. I had already been on a soul searching, transformational journey for several years at that point, but I had yet to master my anxiety. I was learning to take control of my own life and becoming president would be a brave, defiant step that would continue to move me in the right direction.

"YES! I'll do it." I was excited and proud and up for the challenge. Of course, it was easy to say that in February, but things quickly got real in June as my term was about to begin. I was finding my way and learning, as all new presidents do. I was feeling optimistic. *Maybe I can do this.* The summer is relatively quiet at the temple, so I had time to get my footing. But with the end of summer approaching, the Jewish holidays were almost upon us.

Writing the speech was the first hurdle. I didn't consider myself a writer. Many of my synagogue colleagues were the literary, intellectual, academic types, and my style was more, stream of consciousness writing. My writing reflected my personality and what and how I think and speak. I was unable to deliver a polished, eloquent, and captivating speech. I got the feeling that the few who reviewed my speech prior to me delivering it, thought it was juvenile and elementary, but I tried not to let their perceived opinions discourage me. I was quite pleased with how it had turned out. It conveyed my message perfectly. It was an open and honest representation of who I was and "the financial ask" portion of the speech was toned down. I had to be me. If there's one thing I have never been, it's a phony. After all, everyone knew the purpose of the speech, and I was hoping my words would inspire them to reach into their pockets without directly saying "we need your money."

There was a service the night before the big day, and I lingered after most people had left, so I could practice from the pulpit and podium where I would be standing the next morning. The immediate former president and I had been chatting, and she asked if she could stay and hear the speech. I really didn't want her to, but how could I say no? Her style was completely different from mine, and I couldn't bear any criticism this late in the game since I was already filled with dread.

I described the terror that I was experiencing to her in great detail, and she was surprised by it. She figured that it would be no big deal for me since I was chatty and outgoing. WRONG. My voice was trembling as I began to read from the pages that I was gripping tightly. You could see the handprints on each page as I turned to reveal the next. My mouth was as dry as cotton, and I could barely produce enough saliva to get through the seven or eight-minute speech.

When I was done, the former president was kind and supportive and told me she thought it was great. She specifically pointed out the parts that really touched her heart, and I wanted to grab her and squeeze her as tightly as I had done to the pages in my hands a few minutes earlier. As we turned out the lights and exited the synagogue for the night, I tried calming myself down, reminding myself that tomorrow at this time it would all be over. My dad would often utter those words to me when I was anxious over something, so I figured I'd give it a try since he was partially responsible for getting me into this mess in the first place.

I went home and practiced reading while occasionally looking up to make eye contact with my pretend audience during different parts of the speech. I had read it enough to feel comfortable with it, so I put the pages down and went up to bed. Somehow, I actually slept. You would have thought that I would be up all night worrying, but I wasn't. There was a lot of soothing, self-talk going on in my head. I must have gotten so bored listening to it that it put me to sleep.

The minute my eyes popped open the next morning, I could feel the internal trembling begin. *Why the heck did I agree to this? What possessed me to think I could do this? This is a horrific idea!* Certainly not the best thoughts to begin the day.

I took a shower, did my makeup and hair with such precision that you'd think I was going to be examined and graded for the job I had done. I felt confident in how I looked, and I read the speech once more before getting in my car to drive the few short miles over to the temple.

As an officer, we would arrive an hour early to be there to greet the congregants as they entered the building. This had always been one of my favorite responsibilities. I had done it for years and it was special to now be representing the congregation as its president. I was feeling very proud of myself, at least in those moments. Once everyone was inside and the service began, I knew I had approximately eighty minutes until it would be my turn to stand and walk up to take my place on the pulpit.

Just the idea of having all eyes on me, walking from my seat in the audience to the pulpit, was enough to make me feel sick. 150 pairs of eyes watching my every move, looking at my clothes, hair, legs, etc. I thought I had repaired all those feelings of insecurity and unworthiness, but obviously not. As the service progressed, I started feeling seriously sick to my stomach. *What if I lose my cookies right here in front of everyone? Maybe I should go to the bathroom and then text the Rabbi and send him my apologies. I could tell him I was ill and had to leave. My speech is already on the podium, so he could read it for me.* I knew I would never do that, but it was nice to fantasize.

Suddenly, it was time, and he was introducing me. *Here goes nothing.*

It's quite a different perspective looking at the congregation from the pulpit, versus my nice, comfy, invisible seat in the congregation. As I opened my mouth to say, "Shana Tova" (wishing people a good year) the words seemed to get caught up in my saliva-less mouth. I then began to read, trying to contain the trembling in both my voice and my body. I was sure that it was insanely obvious just how frightened I was at that moment, but my only choice was to forge on.

My first couple of paragraphs contained a few sentences that were meant to be light and funny, and happily I looked up to see people smiling and chuckling. *Wow! They're listening. I'm clearly doing okay.* The speech began by explaining why I had decided to become president. I didn't reveal the fear factor, that part wasn't ready for prime time just yet. I shared that my dad's own journey in temple life had been one of the reasons I had accepted the role.

As I was telling the story, I mentioned that he had passed away years ago and two very unexpected things happened. The first was that I choked up. All the times I had practiced the speech this had never happened. Being up on that pulpit, speaking to the congregation as its president, thinking about my dad, delivered a feeling, an emotion, a moment I had not anticipated. I had to pause before I was able to continue talking. Tears began to well in my eyes as I desperately tried to contain them. I looked out into the congregation, and what I saw changed my life forever.

The second unexpected thing that happened was I saw others with tears in their eyes. I had everyone's attention. No one was fidgeting or looking down at their lap, the floor, or their phone. They were engaged. They were hearing and feeling what I was saying. My words were impacting them. My elementary, regular person, nothing fancy words were touching them. I went from trembling to soaring. Soaring with confidence and pride. I never wanted the feeling to end. *How had I lived for fifty-five years and never felt anything like this before?*

Once the service ended, there was a receiving line, which I, as president, participated in. One person after another told me how my speech had touched them. They shared how my story made them think of their own stories. Some said it was the best speech (at least by our temple president's) that they had ever heard. It was surreal listening to their praise and accolades. I was beaming and bursting with pride. I stood there in a dream-like state soaking in each and every moment.

The next day while still basking in the afterglow, I realized I had to do this again in ten days. Part of me couldn't wait that long to get back up there, while another piece of me once again felt fear. Not the same fear as a few days earlier, but now I set the standard. I had gone and set the bar too high. All these people are now expecting me to be moving and inspirational every time I speak. Chances were good that I was a one hit wonder.

The speech writing didn't flow for me as easily as it had the first time since I was now experiencing performance anxiety. After a few different stops and starts, I settled on a second product I was proud of. My heart still raced during the service, waiting for the Rabbi to introduce me, however, it wasn't beating quite as fast as it had been a week earlier. This time I had to ask a bit more directly for money, so it wasn't as emotional. I still received compliments while standing in line but now they sounded a bit different. Initially, the comments were that of amazement. People were surprised at my ability to convey a powerful, heartfelt message. Now the compliments were more matter of fact, "Wow! You're really good at this!"

I couldn't believe I had to wait an entire year to do it all again.

In just ten short days, I had become a completely different person.

♥ 26 ♥

Keeping an Open Mind

"Keep your mind open to change all the time. Welcome it. Court it. It is only by examining and reexamining your opinions and ideas that you can progress." —Dale Carnegie

I'm a music lover. My most favorite place to listen is in my car where I can sing at the top of my lungs and not care how I sound. Of course, I have gotten the occasional stare when stopped at a light, and I'm singing like I'm on stage performing, but it doesn't bother me since I'll never see that stranger again.

A couple of my friends would tell me about a podcast that they were listening to. At first, I didn't understand what a podcast was. I couldn't imagine how it worked. *Who are these people? What are they talking about that was so interesting to listen to? How do you even search to find a podcast that might be of interest to you?* I was curious, so I asked Mary to show me how you find and listen to these podcast people.

I was shocked at how easy it was, but really didn't want to give up my career as a singing driver, since I had no other time to listen to music. So I forgot about podcasts, at least for the moment, and continued belting out the tunes. Several months later, an email I read rocked my world and motivated me to start exploring this new (at least new to me) world of podcasts.

I don't recall who the author of this email was since I somehow had wound up on hundreds of email lists, but it changed my life. The email talked about the regrets that many people have on their deathbed. At first glance, I thought it was too morbid and almost didn't continue reading, but I did. The email listed the common regrets of dying people such as:

- Living a life that was unfulfilling
- Never chasing after their dreams
- Not taking better care of their bodies and overall well-being
- Not giving back to the people and world around them
- Choosing work that lacked meaning for them

As I was reading, I began to picture myself as an old woman about to die, reflecting on my life. *Will I have these same regrets?* I certainly would right now if my last day on earth was today. That realization scared me to death. I've got only one chance at this game of life. This is my one and only life and I don't want to have any regrets. I felt like Ebenezer Scrooge when he woke up on Christmas morning. I'd been given a gift and the clock was ticking. I needed to get started turning this ship around immediately.

And so, my journey into the world of podcasts began.

I sampled a variety of shows, searching for ones about weight loss and self-improvement. I would hear an interview and wind up checking out the podcast of the interviewee. I had absolutely no idea that there were so many people out there dedicated to helping others and it was all free. The more I listened and learned, the more I believed that I did have the power to change my life, even at this stage of the game, in my late fifties when most people would be soon planning their retirement.

Figuring out how to begin to change was the most difficult part. There were so many different areas of my life that needed attention, which made it overwhelming and hard to decide where to focus my attention. In the end, my health won out. It seemed like a logical place to begin since being healthy would increase my odds of living longer, which in turn would buy me more time to live the life that I've always wanted. There was just one problem. I didn't know what that life looked like.

I had already lost a considerable amount of weight and was still working at losing more. I decided to change course and focus on my stress and mental health, something I never really considered doing before. During different difficult times in my life, I had spoken to different therapists. It was helpful, but I was not in therapy at the time.

As I ventured into the world of personal development (I didn't even know there was such a thing) I would hear many people utilizing similar techniques. Meditation was something that everyone seemed to be doing. In my wildest dreams, I had never ever considered meditating. I thought only hippies meditated, so I was shocked to learn that wasn't the case at all. I decided to give it a try.

Of course, I had absolutely no idea how to meditate, so I downloaded a popular app on my phone. I sat down, turned on the meditation, which consisted of spa music and a man's voice reminding me to breathe in and out and focus on the breath. *What good is that?* I needed a lot more help than I was getting. I would close my eyes and feel like I was going to jump out of my skin just sitting there. This seemed like a tremendous waste of time. All I wanted to do was open my eyes and get on with my day.

But I forced myself to sit there for the beginner's three-minute recording. I struggled to focus on my breathing. Instead, my mind was chatting up a storm, either telling me this was a ridiculous idea or listing all the things I should be doing instead of sitting around with my eyes closed, wasting precious time. This was such a dumb idea. I wondered how anyone believed this was a good use of time.

Yet I was determined, so I tried a different app. This time I chose one where the person guided you throughout the entire meditation without leaving it all up to you. I found this to be a lot easier and I loved that you could choose from a library of topics and length of meditations. Having a voice other than my own, guiding me was extremely helpful. Whenever I would get off track, the calm voice would remind me to bring my thoughts back to the present.

I found myself looking forward to meditating. I began to try longer meditations by increasing the time in small increments. I pushed myself to do a ten-day meditation challenge that the app community was doing together. I got excited to see the stars pop up in the app as I completed each day.

Before I knew it, I was an official meditator, and I was proud of myself. No one else even knew I was doing this. I was no longer looking for others' approval. I approved of myself, and I was starting to see how that was enough—there was nothing better. Now that I had the bug, I was anxious to further my journey into this new world. My next move was not consciously planned, it just sort of happened.

I tried yoga, which was a *huge* deal for me. I had been seeing a pain management doctor for several years due to my back and nerve pain. At age thirty-six, I had the spinal fusion and then eleven and thirteen years later, respectively, had each hip replaced. Even after the surgeries, I was still experiencing pain. Each visit, my doctor would tell me the same things: lose weight, do yoga, and swim. As you know, I was always working on the weight part, but I outright refused to try the other two recommendations.

This tall, thin, male doctor had no idea what he was asking of me. I had seen what those women looked like coming out of a yoga studio and none of them looked like me. They were all thin and were clearly made to wear tight fitting yoga pants and tank tops. I was sure that every one of them could twist and turn their bodies into a pretzel, something my fused and fake body could never do. There was no way I was setting myself up to be embarrassed and judged. Next suggestion … swimming.

But swimming was a hassle. You had to change your clothes into a bathing suit (which was its own problem). After you were done, you would need to dry off, change, dry your hair, and possibly apply your makeup. The effort was not worth it. The idea of getting wet and just swimming back and forth under water was completely unappealing. Not to mention, I hadn't truly swum in so many years that I didn't remember how. Swimming was officially out.

I had a couple of friends who did yoga almost every day and they would try convincing me to give it a try. Of course, I told them what I told myself, "I don't do yoga. Yoga is not for me." This was my standard answer, until a new yoga studio opened around the corner from my house. My friends joined and told me that the classes were basically empty. I was a bit more confident in my appearance since losing weight, and decided, if I was ever going to give this a try, this was the perfect opportunity. I agreed but was scared out of my mind.

This wasn't a regular yoga class, but hot yoga, which was a new yoga trend that made this idea even more appalling. I struggled to find an outfit that was both yoga appropriate and made me feel comfortable in my own skin. I was second guessing this decision, even as I pulled open the door to the studio. Unfortunately, the teacher was waiting right inside the vestibule to greet me, so there was no turning back. I explained to her all my physical ailments and impairments and stressed to her that I had never done yoga before. I wanted to make sure her expectations were as low as possible.

The heat smacked me in the face the moment I opened the door to the yoga studio. I was sweating, and I hadn't even unrolled my mat. I realized I hadn't given the hot feature enough consideration. Now I became concerned about not being able to breathe during the class, let alone do the poses. As always, the idea seemed like a good one, until I was in the situation.

As class started the teacher told us to begin in child's pose. I watched my friend to see what she was doing and tried to make my body do the same. The teacher explained that any time we needed to, we could always rest in this position called child's pose. *Rest? She considers this rest?* My thighs were burning, my shoulders were on fire, and my butt was sticking up in the air. The instructor did come around and gently pushed on my rear end to try and get it closer to my legs. I almost sprung up off my mat when I felt her hands on me. However, I didn't have the physical ability to spring up, so I just laid there in misery while sweat dripped into my eyes.

I spent the next hour trying to get into and hold all the different poses, but by the time I got into the pose, or whatever my version of the pose was, we were already moving to another. I couldn't keep up. At times, we would be in downward dog, and she would instruct us to hang out there to recover. *If I can't rest in a child's pose, how the heck can I rest in a downward facing dog?* My arms hurt so much that I couldn't even stay in that position for more than a few seconds. All I could think about was when would this class end. I hated that there was no clock in the room, which I assumed was on purpose so that you wouldn't be able to see just how much longer you would be tortured.

Once we were instructed to lay on our backs in a shavasana pose, I prayed this was the end. Clearly, there was a reason class ended in this dead man's pose because yoga was obviously a killer. Lying on my back had never felt so good. It was a reward after putting myself through an hour of hell. Now I had to decide whether I should lie or tell the truth when the teacher and my friend asked how I liked it. I decided on a hybrid answer explaining how the class had been very challenging and left me feeling exhausted, but in a good way. I guess that was kind of the truth.

My back felt great. The stretching and heat really did do wonders for my pain. I hated the fact that my doctor might have been right. This was quite a conundrum. I didn't see how I could ever drag myself back into that torture chamber again. I was honest with my friend and told her how embarrassed and uncomfortable I had been. She couldn't really understand because she was one of those skinny yoga ladies. She had no concept of how inadequate the class had made me feel.

Even if she didn't quite get it, she reminded me that I shouldn't care about what others think. She told me that she pays no attention to anyone else during class. Instead, she is solely focused on herself and her abilities. I hoped that others would do the same. However, even if I convinced myself that others would not be judging me, I would still be judging myself. The class had made me feel incredibly uncomfortable and deficient. I had been chastising myself during the class.

I needed to focus on the benefits. I had lived with back pain for over a decade and longed for relief. Maybe I *could* do yoga. In a moment of clarity, I joined the yoga studio. I became an official member. I forced myself to attend at least two classes a week. I would always try and figure out which classes were least attended and go to those. As I sampled the classes, I discovered that not all instructors were alike and found a few who I liked and who made me feel comfortable.

Yoga became part of my life, although I still had to really psych myself up to attend class. It got a little easier once I became familiar with the terms and alternative poses that worked better for my body. At least, I knew what was going on and didn't tremble with fear each time the instructor gave us a directive. I found myself looking forward to attending class. Although, I wasn't really looking forward to doing yoga, but instead loved the after-effects on my body. I liked the way my body felt as I eased into savasana. I started to notice a difference in my pain level. Even though I really wanted to, I couldn't deny it. The doctor was right. Yoga was good for my back.

As the membership at the studio grew, they began to add more classes, including a 5:30 a.m. class, three days a week. I couldn't even imagine who would want to get up at 5 a.m., drive to the studio and take class. I liked to sleep as late as I possibly could without being late to work. Something about the early morning class kept popping up in my head at the oddest times. I realized I was fighting with myself. The angel on my shoulder was trying hard to convince me that attending the class would be a wonderful way to start my day. It would also free up my evenings and allow me to not have to choose between Jazzercise and yoga. Naturally, the devil on the other shoulder was telling me it was crazy to get up that early in the morning. I was bound to be exhausted the rest of the day.

There was another possible problem with the early morning time. It was who I thought would be attending these classes. Clearly, if you were going to commit to this time, you must be one of those perfect yoga ladies. The ladies who make me feel like I'm not good enough. Who else would be that dedicated to waking up at such a ridiculous hour? The angel and devil would be constantly bickering, and I had to remind myself of the person I was choosing to become, not the person I had been. I reminded myself of how I never wanted to try yoga for so many years, yet now I had incorporated it into my routine. I had to just give it a try and if it didn't work out, at least I could say I tried.

The instructor was new to me, but my friends had raved about her. They told me how challenging her class was and how it was different from the typical yoga flow I had grown to know. *Just great! The torture queen had to be the one teaching this class!* The night before my first 5:30 a.m. class, I barely slept. I was anxious about so many things. First, I was afraid I would sleep through the alarm and not get out of bed. You had to register for this class since it was so early, and I didn't want to be scolded or charged for not attending. My nerves were on high alert, which made sleeping nearly impossible. Secondly, I was extremely anxious about my ability to participate in the class. I didn't want to look or feel inept.

My alarm rang at 5:10 a.m., and I jumped out of bed, brushed my teeth and hair, and put on the clothes I had laid out the night before. Yogi (named for the bear, not yoga), my dog, looked at me like I was crazy as I grabbed my mat and got in my car. There were only a handful of other women there, and I was relieved to see someone else besides myself who didn't look like a perfect yoga lady. I chatted easily with the instructor and shared all my limitations, once again, making sure her expectations were very low.

The room was not as warm as usual since the heat had just been turned on. Now, that was certainly a plus. As class started and the instructor began to prompt us to move in a certain way, I panicked. *Here we go again. She's asking me to do things that my body is just not capable of. I knew this was a bad idea.* As my blood pressure and pulse rose, the instructor approached me. My body immediately stiffened. She whispered in my ear, giving me alternative moves and asking if I was comfortable trying them. *Wow with a capital W!* No one had ever taken the time to do this. Immediately, I relaxed and knew I had finally found just what I needed. A person who wanted to take the time to understand how my body moves. I had stumbled upon one of the best instructors there was. She was skilled and knew precisely how to adapt her teaching methods to meet the individual needs of each student.

For a year and a half, three of us became the regular 5:30 a.m. crew. Others would come and go, but we were the core group. The four of us, including the instructor, were a cohesive, supportive unit. A group that I looked forward to seeing every Monday, Wednesday, and Friday. We loved it so much that we tried to convince the instructor to hold class five days a week. The last few months, we added a meditation component to our workout. The meditation was in silence, and

I fought it at first but then found if I let myself go, it was amazing how rested and peaceful I felt when we were done. I absolutely loved our 5:30 a.m. group and would have attended forever. Unfortunately, it came to a screeching halt when the pandemic hit and by the time we got back to real life, everyone had scattered.

I continued part of my early morning yoga routine from home by watching various instructors on YouTube, however, I rarely chose an hour-long class. It felt too long and was unenjoyable. I convinced myself that something was better than nothing and settled on a twenty-minute class to start my morning, typically around 6 a.m. I would then meditate, so I had developed a nice little morning routine. Once again, it was time to try something new. The pandemic was a perfect time to experiment since there was nowhere to run to each day. It gave me plenty of time to experiment.

Next up was journaling. I had heard so many people on podcasts mention their journaling habit. Everyone seemed to have their unique spin on how and what they do, so it was hard for me to figure out which method would work best for me. After a little research, I landed on the type of journal that had prompts and would help me organize my day and accomplish my daily tasks. I bought a journal that allowed me to list and prioritize my to-do list. It also gave me space to write things I was grateful for. This is hard to admit, but I found this intimidating. *How can I come up with something unique to be grateful for each day? Once I ran through the list of people, I'm grateful for, I'm about tapped out. What else can I write?*

It also had a space to write down affirmations. I had absolutely no idea how to begin to write an affirmation and thought it sounded a bit too hippie for me, but I reminded myself that I needed to keep an open mind. So I searched and found hundreds of examples of affirmations, so there was no need to reinvent the wheel. Each day I would choose three of them and write them in my journal. I often would repeat the ones that really resonated with me. There was no law that said they needed to be different each day. I had to constantly remind myself that I would not be handing this in for a grade. No one else is seeing my journal other than me.

I bought myself neon-colored index cards and each day after completing my journal, I would write my top daily priorities, as well as my affirmations, on a card. I'd tape the card to my computer monitor so that it was in front of me most of the time. I was amazed at just how quickly this practice began to impact my day. I accomplished more and was constantly reminded of my big picture goals when I read those affirmations repeatedly. My morning routine had grown and was now taking a little over an hour to complete before I even got into the shower. My alarm rang earlier and earlier each morning to accommodate my longer routine.

I was really pleased with myself. I had begun to change my day, and in turn, my life, one step at a time. I felt the metamorphosis happening, and it was exhilarating. My morning routine became the backbone of my life, one that I rarely missed. I didn't know if it was possible or necessary to add anything more. After all, I decided that getting up any earlier than 5 a.m. was ridiculous, so instead, I experimented with different types of meditation and journaling. I also started to watch different yoga videos, just to spice things up a bit. Even with my newly formed open mind, I was leery to give free form journaling a try.

The idea of taking out a blank piece of paper and pen with no prompts or instructions was intimidating. *What the heck am I supposed to write? Should I just list my goals and affirmations as I was already doing?* That seemed to defeat the whole purpose. *Am I supposed to start with "Dear Diary?"* I read that I should write whatever comes to mind. My mind was blank from fear. Fear that I didn't know what I was doing, or I wasn't going to do it right. I decided that I would write whatever I was thinking about, including fear. Once I started writing, the words and sentences started flowing. It was flowing so quickly that my pen couldn't keep up with my thoughts. I wrote three full pages without stopping, and once I was done, I sat back and let out a big sigh.

I was absolutely shocked with how good that had felt. I was stunned by the words that had made it onto the page. My writing had started with one idea and somehow a page in, I was talking about something completely different that I hadn't even known had been on my mind. This was a very different experience than I had imagined. It was therapeutic. I had discovered a form of therapy I didn't even know I needed or was available to me. I couldn't wait to write again the next day.

I had always thought I didn't enjoy writing. In school it was far from my favorite subject. I was a math girl who couldn't relate to the more creative types. I had been convinced that I did not have a creative bone in my body, but my love of journaling allowed me to see that maybe there was something a little creative somewhere deep down inside of me. A side of me that I had never discovered or allowed myself to discover. I never would have imagined that at my age (late fifties) this was even possible.

I had to remind myself of how my life had begun to change, just because now, I was keeping an open mind. I was excited about what I would try next. In my wildest dreams, I never would have imagined the possibilities that awaited me— now that I had discovered the power of, "Maybe I can."

On second thought... maybe I can!

♥ 27 ♥

Gary's MDS Diagnosis

"A great relationship doesn't happen because of the love you had in the beginning, but how well you continue building love until the end." – Anonymous

Gary's health continued to decline after he stopped working. For several years, his gastroenterologist was telling him to go and see a liver specialist. He felt it was necessary due to his blood work results. Gary being Gary, blew it off. I was not attending many of his doctor appointments with him because I needed to be at the office during the day, so I was only getting the information Gary wanted to share with me. He often didn't share everything because he knew I would nag him if he wasn't doing what he was told.

He never seemed to schedule his own doctor appointments, so I took it upon myself to do it because if I didn't, he would never go. Sometimes, at the last minute I would have to cancel the appointment. Gary would tell me he was too anxious to go, or he wasn't feeling well. I seemed to spend part of my days making appointments, canceling appointments, and rescheduling appointments. Occasionally, I would insist on taking him, so I could hear what was really going on and ask any questions I had.

Another benefit of taking him was that he didn't have to drive. He had become a lousy driver. He hit mailboxes and retaining walls. His minivan had dents and scratches all over it. Money was tight, so we never had anything repaired. Even if we could spend the money, it seemed impractical, given the likelihood that he would collide with something else again. I would leave work early to come home and pick him up and learn that he wasn't awake, or he would tell me he was unable to go.

I was living in a state of constant anger and frustration—not a good way to live. I was stuck in a miserable loop and didn't know how to get out. Many of my friends and family asked why I didn't get divorced. They loved Gary but saw how his behavior was negatively affecting me. I became impatient with him and resented what he was doing to me. I busied myself with so many different volunteer positions and exercise classes, so I would only basically be home to sleep, this way I could avoid being around him. His behavior was also negatively impacting Sam and Ben. They needed his love and support, yet he found it hard to get off his train of misery. He no longer could think about anyone or anything else other than himself and his problems.

Divorce never felt like an option for a variety of reasons. The main reason was that I did still love Gary—even though I disliked him tremendously at the time. He required a lot of help, and if I decided to get divorced, the responsibility would fall on the boys' shoulders. I never, *ever* wanted that for them since I knew firsthand how difficult that was. Money was another issue. I couldn't afford to pay for one home, let alone two, and I didn't want any added financial stress. I had enough stress as it was. I was sticking with him regardless of what happened, but I didn't really know how I would survive.

Gary's behavior began to change. He was angrier and sullener. His wonderful sense of humor seemed to have been replaced by a permanent frown. The man I had married was gone. He was still physically with me, but his vibrant, easy-going, loving personality had disappeared. He was quick to anger, and when he wasn't complaining or moaning, he was sleeping. There were days when I couldn't get him out of bed. It started out as one day in bed and grew to several days, sometimes five or six days in a row.

Sam begged me to do something. I had pleaded with Gary to check himself into a psychiatric hospital to get the help he needed, but my pleas fell on deaf ears. I found myself running home from work after receiving a call from Sam, who was upset by Gary's anger that was often directed at him. I spoke to Gary's psychiatrist who gave me advice on who to call and what to expect if Gary didn't agree to go to the hospital. I decided it was time. Gary had been in bed for several days and his destructive patterns were just repeating themselves. I called the number for mental health mobile response. After speaking to me, they determined that it was necessary to come out to the house and speak to Gary.

A young man came and spoke to him briefly, but Gary was not being very cooperative. The man explained to me that there was nothing he could do. Gary was clearly very depressed, but he refused treatment. He further explained that Gary did not seem to be in danger of harming himself or others, so there was no legal reason to bring him into the hospital against his will. I explained that Gary is slowly killing himself by not taking his medication properly. He refused to eat or take medicine those days when he was hunkered down in bed with the covers over his head. The answer I got was, basically, that there was nothing that could be done, and so he walked out the door.

What am I to do now? Sam was clearly suffering, and so was I. Ben was away at school, so he only knew what I was telling him. This was no way for any of us to live. I called the mobile response number again a few weeks later and had a long discussion with a different person. He agreed with me that something had to give, and he gave me some tips on what to say and do the next time I felt it was time to call. That time came just a few weeks later, on the sixth, consecutive day of Gary being in bed. A different person came to the house to speak with Gary this time. Once again, he refused treatment.

However, the woman who had come to the house felt he needed to be assessed and, this time, legally, there was cause to bring him to the hospital. She called the police and ambulance and explained her decision to Gary. He was angry but seemed to accept it. He got out of bed and did what he could to prepare himself. He willingly got in the ambulance, and I jumped in my car and followed.

Gary had begun to cry the minute we got into the hospital. The crying never stopped unless he fell asleep. We were brought to a private room in the emergency room where we were waiting for a psychiatrist to evaluate him. An aide also sat in the room with us. Her job was to note what Gary was saying and doing and to make sure he wasn't trying to hurt himself. Occasionally, I tried to explain to him the difference between him agreeing to stay in the hospital, in the psychiatric unit, versus a doctor legally forcing him to stay. If he voluntarily agreed, he would be transferred to the small psychiatric ward in our local hospital, if not, he could be shipped off to any psychiatric hospital in the state.

But he still wouldn't agree. He assumed a doctor would not commit him, and he and I would just go home after this ordeal was over. There was no psychiatrist on duty, so we met with a tele psych. A social worker wheeled a TV into the room and Gary, and I virtually met with the doctor. Gary was able to stop the crying long enough to try and tell the doctor he didn't want or need to stay. Then the doctor asked to speak to me. He asked for my opinion and Gary shot me a look that screamed "you'd better not tell him I should stay." I wondered how this doctor could put me in this position. I told him that, although I didn't want Gary to stay, I felt he desperately needed the help. The doctor agreed.

Gary was committed, meaning he was legally forced to be admitted into a psychiatric hospital. He was furious and upset. I begged him to tell the social worker that he agreed to stay. He was terrified of being sent to a strange place. The social worker explained that it was too late now that a doctor had already committed him. I begged her to just try and see if he was allowed to change his mind, so he could stay in this hospital, and she said she would try. We waited for hours to find out what would happen next. Gary continued to sob, drifting off to sleep for a few minutes only to then wake up and continue crying.

Eventually, the social worker came back and told us she had done it. Gary was able to stay in our local hospital's small psychiatric unit. Even though Gary was grateful, he was still in the depths of despair. I left him sobbing as I watched him being rolled away from me. Tears flowed down my face as a tremendous sigh of relief escaped through my mouth. All the events of the day seemed to sink in now that the immediate crisis had ended. I needed to regain my strength for whatever lay ahead.

The next day, I was allowed to visit Gary for a half hour. A nurse instructed me to sit down on a specific couch and told me she would get Gary. Gary entered the room in a hospital gown and was still sobbing. He and I could barely have a conversation. He was unable to rationally speak and just kept crying and telling me how sad he was. My heart was breaking as I watched and listened to him. His pain and suffering were palpable, and I couldn't fix it. I was helpless.

Selfishly, I was glad that I was only allowed to see him for a half an hour a day. It was too difficult to see him like that for any longer, and if I couldn't do anything to help him, there was no point. I braced myself the next day as my visiting time approached. This time when Gary walked into the room, I realized he wasn't sobbing. He was much calmer and seemed almost hopeful. It felt like it had been years since he was hopeful and positive. He told me he felt better, and that he had attended a therapy group and had learned about the importance of breathing.

Our visit flew by and I left feeling encouraged. My next few visits brought more of the same. *Who is this man?* He loved therapy, something he had always refused to try in the past and he was doing arts and crafts. I was completely blown away and excited—excited about the future. My husband had resurfaced and had resurfaced as a more positive, open man than he had been before. It was remarkable.

After a week, he was released and began a virtual therapy program for three hours a day, three days a week. He became the star of the group. He was upbeat and happy. He was extremely supportive of the other members and was constantly contributing to the group discussions. His outlook on life had completely changed. All the hard decisions I had to make to force him to get the help he needed, had been the right ones.

The atmosphere in the house became lighter and more uplifting. It was no longer difficult to stay there. It was comfortable and inviting. Gary still struggled with anxiety, but the depression had lifted. I tried to do whatever I could to lower his anxiety levels, but sometimes I just wasn't able to help. He tried employing the new strategies he was learning, even if it wasn't always successful.

I really put his newfound success to the test when I planned on taking a three-night trip to Las Vegas for the company's 100th anniversary celebration. I had been looking forward to this for a very long time. Joan was going to accompany me, as she had in the past, and it was a once in a lifetime opportunity I didn't want to miss. Gary knew how much it meant to me and made a monumental effort to overcome his anxiety so I could attend. I was excited to be going but also had a nagging feeling in my gut that I was making a mistake.

We arrived in Las Vegas on a Sunday afternoon and had a relaxing, fun first night in town. At 5 a.m. the next morning, my phone rang. It was Gary's doctor's office. The doctor needed to speak to us regarding blood work that Gary had just done that previous Friday. It seemed his white blood cell count was alarmingly low. The doctor recommended that we repeat the test just to verify the accuracy of the results.

I arranged for my friend Barbara to pick him up and drive him to the lab that afternoon. That evening, I hardly slept. I was sure this was the beginning of the end. I assumed Gary's liver disease had progressed. I had researched the disease and had often wondered when we would see a distinct change in his condition. I was up all night with my mind racing with thoughts of Gary dying, how the boys would handle it, and what plans I needed to make. I then felt guilty for even thinking that way. I told myself that I was clearly jumping to conclusions. I needed to stay positive.

The second blood test verified that the results were accurate and with the help of Gary's doctor, we got an appointment with the hematologist two days later. The appointment was on the day I was flying home. I hoped to be able to join the appointment by phone but was in the air at that time, so Mindy took him and taped the conversation for me. The hematologist wasn't quite as alarmed as Gary's internist. She thought it might be due to a medication change, but Gary couldn't remember the name of his new medications, and I had forgotten to give that information to him, so she couldn't be sure.

The doctor recommended that we make another appointment the following week when I could attend. She asked that I let her know the name of the new medications, so she could research their side effects, which I did. A couple of days after I arrived home, I became ill with COVID- 19, so, once again, I could not attend the hematologist appointment. Ben drove Gary, and I joined via telephone. The doctor said that the new medications Gary was taking would not affect his white blood cell count. She recommended doing a bone marrow biopsy, and said she had availability to do it right away.

Gary started to hesitate, but the doctor and I coerced him into biting the bullet and doing it right then and there, which he did. It would be ten to fourteen days until the results were in. Those ten to fourteen days felt more like a year. Once again, I turned to the internet to see what disease might be causing Gary's low blood count. Gary and I were both convinced that it had to be due to the liver, and not a blood disorder, but we needed that confirmation.

Results day finally arrived. We had to meet with the doctor online because I was still not allowed in their office due to their COVID restrictions. As the doctor started talking, she started off by telling us how surprised she had been with the results. I wasn't sure if it was a good surprise or a bad surprise, but it quickly became evident that it was the latter. She mentioned some long, complicated disease that neither of us had ever heard of. It was myelodysplastic syndrome (MDS), considered a type of precancerous disease of the blood.

As the doctor continued to talk, I picked up my phone and started googling to try and get a better idea of what this all meant, to see if there was something specific that I should be asking. She continued to explain that instead of the disease having stages, as most types of cancer do, this disease was categorized by the level of risk. Unfortunately, Gary's results showed a high-risk level. He had one of the more aggressive forms of this disease.

Gary and I were speechless.

A few years prior, Gary had been diagnosed with non-alcoholic liver cirrhosis. We knew that between that disease, his diabetes, and Crohn's disease, his blood work would often be abnormal. We had been convinced that this time was no different. I asked the doctor if the MDS was related to any of his other diseases, and she said it wasn't. I reiterated and asked again, "You mean this diagnosis is in addition to the others?" She shook her head yes.

She then went on to explain that the only possible cure was a stem cell transplant, but unfortunately, due to Gary's other illness', he was not a candidate. There was a type of low dose chemotherapy that he could do in the hopes of extending his life. Neither of us could believe what we were hearing. I had an out of body experience. This was happening to someone else, not us. It was completely unexpected. Both Gary and I were so sure that the wacky blood numbers were related to his liver.

Once we got off the call, I began the trip down the Google rabbit hole. I searched for countless combinations of diagnoses, treatments, and survival rates. Neither of us had asked how long he had to live. It was something we weren't ready to face. We needed time to just digest the news. My investigation led me to believe that Gary's life expectancy was nine to fifteen months. I started to process the idea that I would become a widow.

Although Gary had been difficult to live with, the fact is I still loved him. He had been my partner for almost thirty years. Memories came flooding back, and I relived all the happy moments we shared. I couldn't imagine my life without him. I loved being married. I loved having a partner. Even though our relationship had certainly changed significantly over the past several years, I still had him to discuss problems and ideas with. There was not another person in this world who knew me as well as Gary did. I couldn't bear the thought of losing my life partner.

Initially, he had a good attitude, thanks to his miraculous shift after his psychiatric hospitalization. He told the doctor that we were a team, and he was going to fight his hardest. I was both impressed and pleasantly surprised at his determination. I had so many different questions for the doctor now that I had some time to research and think. Most of them involved a timeline, but she said that she hated giving any kind of numbers or percentages. Each person is unique, and she didn't want to put anything in our heads. I understood her point, but I couldn't stand that she wouldn't give us a clue or a range.

Gary began chemotherapy with his fighting attitude intact. Chemotherapy does typically lower your immune system, but with Gary, it dropped dangerously low. He wound up in sepsis and was almost admitted to the ICU for an infection that began from a tiny cut on the tip of his thumb. He was in severe pain and miserable. After several days in the hospital, we were told he needed surgery to remove a pocket of the infection that was not responding to the antibiotics. His MDS diagnosis complicated matters, and it was decided it would be best to have Gary transferred to a higher-level hospital.

All the fight and positivity Gary had displayed just a few weeks earlier had flown out the window. He was miserable and the whole thing wound up to be a terrible, stressful ordeal for both of us. I was at the hospital with him every day for eight to twelve hours. I was there advocating for him. He was back to being angry and depressed, and I spent much of my time trying to get him to calm down. He wasn't even aware that I was no longer able to go to work. I couldn't bear the thought of leaving him lying there all alone. I would have wanted to be there regardless of his MDS diagnosis, but knowing his life was being cut short left me no choice but to stay by his side.

Thankfully, the team of women at my office were outstanding. They handled everything. All I needed to do was check my emails and remember to pay them. Without those women, I never could have been able to be there for Gary. He came home after three weeks and wound up back in the hospital just five days later to be treated for a subsequent infection that had formed from fluid retention in his legs. He was not happy and was tough to deal with. He was yelling at me and everyone else, including the nurses and doctors.

During the first hospitalization, a psychiatrist needed to be brought in, since Gary's anger and anxiety had become extreme. He began taking new medication, but it wasn't helping. If I thought he was difficult to deal with while hospitalized the first time, it was hard to believe that his mood could get any worse. It became unbearable. While I was visiting him during the second hospitalization, I just kept hoping and praying that he would fall asleep, so I could get a break from listening to him.

Once he came home, his mood didn't improve much. He was miserable, especially when he first woke up. There was a lot of crying and moaning, which was also accompanied by anger and meanness. I tried to anticipate his needs, so I wouldn't have to be the victim of his verbal barrage, but it was usually unsuccessful.

Several months prior to his diagnosis, we had to turn a small office on the first floor of our house into a bedroom for Gary. Going up the stairs had become difficult for him so this was safer since he had a history of falling.

Our bedroom had never been decorated in the twenty-three years that we had lived there. We always needed whatever money we had for other things. The carpet had been yellow, but it was now sad, stained, and faded. When Gary was still sleeping upstairs, he once fell in the middle of the night directly on his nose. There was blood everywhere, and I was never able to get it out. The carpet made our room look like a crime scene.

I covered the area with towels, so I wouldn't have to see the dried blood each time I walked in the room.

Mindy convinced me that it was finally time to do something just for me. My environment needed a massive upgrade. She and I had a wonderful time picking out carpet, furniture, and blinds. I never used to have any desire to be in my bedroom since it was disgusting. I only went in there to sleep. Once Mindy had worked her magic, my bedroom had become my beautiful oasis. It felt glamorous, indulgent, and calming. Of course, Mindy blew my budget, but I didn't care. She created a place in my home that was just for me.

It was a retreat where I could go to get away from all the crying, moaning, and demands. My bedtime kept getting earlier and earlier, so I could race up those stairs and close the door. My days were now filled with doctor appointments, medication management, and constant trips to the store to get Gary supplies, medication, and food. I continued to barely step foot in my office for months on end. Gary, Sam, and I (Ben was away at school) were all suffering in different ways, and I had to be there to support them both.

Each week seemed to bring some new crisis, challenge, or worry. I struggled with guilt because it seemed ridiculous that Gary should live in such misery for the remainder of his life. If he was going to be in pain and agony, then I would rather see him die sooner. What's the point of living if you're always feeling hopeless, angry, and in pain? My own mental health was suffering, but I was still grateful. Grateful for all the people I had in my life who were there to support and lift me up.

I rarely got a break and could only leave my house to run to the store. I needed something else to focus on other than Gary and Sam. Starting to write this book during that time had become therapeutic. I had been afraid that it would be overwhelming, but instead, it allowed me time to get my mind off my current situation and revisit so many of my life's memories. I would try to schedule an hour a day to write. First thing in the morning worked best because typically no one else would be awake. When I couldn't do that, I would just tell Gary that I had a meeting and retreat to my bedroom oasis with my laptop.

For several months, life continued in a similar, difficult fashion, until Gary's birthday approached. He was turning sixty-five years old. In the past he never really cared about his birthday, which I find crazy since I want the entire world to know when it's my birthday. This year he cared, but not because he wanted to celebrate. The idea that this could be his final birthday hit him hard and days prior to his actual birthday, he retreated to his bed, threw the covers over his head, and wouldn't come out. I dragged him out to a doctor's appointment that he really needed to go to, and they advised him to check himself into the psychiatric ward at the hospital. He refused.

After his birthday, he remained severely depressed. We met online with two other doctors who both recommended hospitalization. Once again, he refused. He missed his therapy appointment, and when I called to let his therapist know, she also recommended hospitalization. I had been down this road just six months earlier and didn't want any of us to have to go through it again. I *begged* him to go to the hospital. He would tell me he would go but "not today." After hearing this answer for three days in a row, I knew it was time. I made the call, once again, to have the mobile response person come out and evaluate him.

The difference between this time and last was drastic. This time Gary wasn't budging. He threatened to punch the poor woman who came out to evaluate him. This was NOT my husband. He never would have threatened to inflict physical harm. The woman had no choice but to call the police. I told Gary what was happening, and he must voluntarily agree to go to the hospital. If he didn't, the police would have to forcefully take him away.

My pleas again fell on deaf ears. Gary was irrational and out of his right mind. The scene that ensued once the six police officers entered our home was horrific. I ran upstairs into my room, hoping not to hear all that was happening, but it was impossible not to hear Gary's yelling. Sam ran downstairs to try and convince Gary to go even after I told him to stay in his room, and I followed him. The police officers asked me to talk to him one more time to try and convince him to go peacefully. I tried, once again, but Gary was screeching at me in a voice I had never heard come out of his mouth.

I ran back upstairs and covered my ears as the six officers had to physically force him onto a stretcher and strap him down. I came downstairs as they were taking him out, and he was screaming that they were hurting him, and his arms were bleeding from the straps. Nothing in my life had prepared me for that moment. I was distraught and afraid. Poor Sam had been there through the whole thing until he eventually couldn't take it and retreated to his room. I hated that I had to leave Sam without really talking to him, but I had to get to the hospital. I had no choice.

The three-week ordeal that followed was excruciating and a reminder of how difficult it is to treat mental illness. For the first few days, Gary was mean and angry. I was mortified by the way he spoke to the nurses, doctors, and me. Some of the aides were afraid to enter his room, and he had an aide sitting in his room twenty-four hours a day recording what he was saying and doing. They were the ones who had no choice but to stay with him and take his abuse. He told me that he hated me and wanted a divorce. There was so much anger and hatred in his eyes when he looked at me. Even though I knew his mind was in an altered state, it still hurt.

I second guessed my decision. *Maybe I jumped the gun and should have waited to call the mobile response team. Maybe he would have eventually checked himself in and would have avoided the traumatic experience of being restrained.* All my friends were very supportive and reassured me that I had done the right thing, but no one could understand how hard this was. It was one of the loneliest feelings in the world. I spent several nights crying alone in my empty house.

Gary's anger subsided for a few days, but his behavior became obsessive and compulsive, and he began having delusions. You couldn't have a logical conversation with him. All he wanted to discuss was whatever obsession was currently on his mind. I was only allowed to visit for half an hour a day, and for many days, all he wanted me to do was bring him a large cheesecake, which he would share with everyone in the psychiatric unit. I tried to explain that bringing food in was forbidden. All the nurses told him as well, but he never really heard what we were saying.

I became truly frightened that this experience had pushed him over the edge. He was experiencing a psychotic break with reality, which had never happened before. *What if he never returned to himself? This was all my fault.* I was petrified that he would have to live out the remainder of his shortened life in an institution. After a couple of weeks, his condition worsened. He began hallucinating and was seeing bugs and mosquitos in his room. He clogged the toilet by flushing paper towels, thinking he was getting rid of the bugs.

He wanted to go home but it was clearly not safe for him or us. To keep him there against his will, the doctors needed to determine if it was legal to do so. It was. This decision required that he be moved to another psychiatric hospital somewhere within the state. After a couple of days, he was moved to a place an hour away from home. He was under the impression he was going home even though several doctors explained to him that he needed further care and would be moved to another facility.

He was placed in a geriatric unit, and I was not permitted to visit him for the first few days. I did speak to the psychiatrist and felt confident that he understood the full picture. He had a plan, but it could take days or weeks to see if Gary would improve. When I was able to speak to Gary, he was miserable and begged me to get him out of there. He was confused, and I couldn't believe all the stories he was telling me. The psychiatrist explained possible long-term solutions if he did not improve. If I felt like I was living in a nightmare, I couldn't bear to imagine how Gary felt.

Miraculously, the medication change worked, and Gary began to return to his "normal" self. In a twenty-four-hour period the discussion had changed from long term commitment to discharge. After one week at the second hospital, Gary was released. Unfortunately, he was still very angry with me and blamed me for absolutely everything. He could barely speak to me without adding a nasty tone or comment. He had trouble sleeping because he was having frequent nightmares about the facility and the other patients and nurses.

I was wracked with guilt. I wrestled with the fact that I was responsible for Gary's mental anguish. Just what a dying man needed, more reason to be anxious. Let me just say that mental illness is the toughest illness I have ever had to deal with. If you have high cholesterol, you take a pill to lower it—nice and simple. With mental illness, everything is a guessing game with lots of trial and error. Psychiatrists take educated guesses but if it's not the right medication or combination of medications, the negative side effects can be scary. After all, these medications alter the brain—something you don't want to mess with.

It took about a week and several sessions with his therapist for Gary to eventually forgive me. I noticed that he was no longer depressed. He was getting out of bed early each day. Once again, Gary was attending a virtual therapy group for nine hours per week. In addition, he made it to his chemotherapy appointments each day on time, which was a first. I was finally able to breathe a sigh of relief.

♥ 28 ♥

Wizard of Oz

"Deliberately seek the company of people who influence you to think and act on building the life you desire."
—Napoleon Hill

My journey into Munchkinland began with a podcast. I didn't exactly know what or who I was interested in listening to, so I started with a subject I knew best—weight. I immediately knew if I connected with the host or not. It's like feeling that connection when you meet someone in person—sometimes, you just know. I landed on a podcast where I wasn't sure whether I loved the host or if she annoyed me. Either way, it was enough to keep me listening.

On one particular episode, she interviewed another woman podcaster, and in her introduction, she acted like this woman was a well-known celebrity. Of course, I had never heard of her. I felt the connection as soon as the woman began to speak. I knew I needed to hear more of what she had to say. Her story resonated with me. She had lost over 150 pounds and at one time had been in a lot of debt. She was straightforward, and it felt like she was speaking directly to me.

I immediately started listening to her podcast. Her words and stories were motivating, and I couldn't get enough. I began listening when I was walking Yogi and while putting my makeup on in the morning. I looked forward to long drives since that would give me the opportunity to listen for extended periods of time. I learned that she had written a book, which I couldn't get my hands on fast enough. I devoured her every word. She was speaking my language.

After several months, the woman began mentioning that her signature, twelve-week course was going to be starting soon. I was intrigued until I saw the price tag. The course was $1,800. I had sticker shock. This seemed like a ridiculous amount of money to spend, especially for someone like me who owed money to everyone, including the IRS. However, that little voice deep in my gut kept nudging me forward. It said that this could be the beginning of something big. The catalyst for the change I now knew I needed and had been longing for.

I was skeptical, wondering whether $1,800 would be worth whatever I was going to get out of this course. As she talked about early bird specials and other discounts, I felt that I was falling prey to classic sales tactics. This was all just a way to get vulnerable people like me to pay her money. I feared I would be making a foolish mistake and spending more money that I didn't have. Once again, my internal voices were arguing with each other, but in the end, I took a leap of faith. I decided that nothing in my life would change unless I changed.

After the first week of the course, I was sure I had made the wrong decision. I hadn't yet been given any life changing information or been told anything that I hadn't already heard her say on the podcast. She did tell everyone to trust the process and not be in a rush. I vowed to give it a try and be patient. By the third week, I noticed a shift in my thinking. I had started to change some of my daily habits, and I noticed that my outlook had begun to shift. I was facing each day with a bit more excitement, despite the difficult circumstances I was living with on a day-to-day basis.

The course was not specifically about money or weight loss, but about overall motivation and methods to change your life. The teachings could be applied to your work, relationships, spiritual health, or any other area of your life you wanted to improve. The hardest part was choosing an area of my life to focus on, without that, it would be too overwhelming. I chose money since that was the one thing that had slowly been eating away at me for most of my life.

For the first time in years, I felt optimistic and hopeful about my future. I was starting to understand that I needed to shift my mindset and perspective and be open to a world of possibility that I never knew existed. Now that I was a believer in the podcaster and her course, I ordered some of the supplement products that she had found helpful. Once again, I had sticker shock when I saw the prices, but I told myself this was all part of my new adventure. I ordered a starter kit, so I could try a variety of items.

The very first day that I drank one of the powders mixed with water, I started feeling a kind of energy that I never had experienced before. I had taken diet pills in the past that would cause my heart to race and make me uncomfortable, but this was nothing like that. I couldn't wait to get to work and start making progress towards my goals. My outlook was even sunnier than usual, and I thought maybe this was a placebo effect. Maybe I wanted it to work so badly, that I was imagining the feelings I experienced.

After a few days, I knew it wasn't my imagination. This stuff really worked, and I wanted to tell everyone I knew about it. Some of my friends tried it and others thought I was nuts. I decided I would sign on to sell the products since I was hyping them up anyway. I sold a couple of things to my friends but wasn't sure how to go about proactively selling. I would go out of my way to avoid network marketers in the past and there I was, now one of them.

As the course progressed, I got nervous about it ending. I was afraid that my old mindset would reappear since I wouldn't have the weekly sessions to support me. The leader would often mention the importance of being in a mastermind group. I had never heard of a mastermind and was clueless as to what exactly they were, how they worked, and who they were for. On one of her podcast episodes, she interviewed the coach who had run the mastermind that she was attending. I now trusted my podcast lady implicitly. If she liked this guy, then he must be good. He said he would be launching a new mastermind group for entrepreneurs, making $0-$500,000 a year. Well, that was me. I was making $0 as a network marketer, maybe this mastermind would teach me how to make money selling the supplements.

I jumped and took another leap of faith by joining the mastermind. There were approximately 150 people in the group, and at the introductory meeting, we were told that the following week we would be broken up into two groups. Each of us would have one minute to introduce ourselves and were asked to share where we needed help as well as what help we could provide to others. I was completely intimidated.

First, after looking at the other 149 faces on zoom, most members were under the age of forty. My age never bothered me before but somehow, I felt old at the age of fifty-seven. They all seemed to be already making money with their businesses. Most of them had some type of coaching business, which I really didn't understand. I had heard of life coaching before but most of these coaches were different. They were coaching people to help with their mindset, money, or social media, just to name a few. They offered online courses, group coaching, or individual coaching.

The vocabulary that was used was all new to me. They were discussing lead magnets, sales funnels, and neuro linguistic programming (NLP). I had stepped into an alternate universe that I never knew existed. I felt like I had discovered that there was life on Mars. I created the tornado by taking a step to join this group, and now I had been dropped into another world, just as Dorothy had been dropped into munchkin land. I didn't know how to act or what to say.

Panic officially set in the day before the next meeting. I wanted to write out my introduction, practice it, and memorize it but there was one problem, I had no idea what to say. I could come up with something for what I needed from the group but what kind of help could I offer? I didn't think that being an auto insurance expert was something this group would find helpful. I decided to be honest and just say that I could help with any insurance question. To justify my statement, I explained how this world was new to me, but if I could be helpful in any way to anyone, I'm here.

I was feeling confident about my presentation, until the introductions began. One by one, as each of these "kids" introduced themselves, I began to lose my nerve. They all seemed to be speaking the same language, a language that I had no knowledge of. That familiar thought popped into my head. I had done it once again. I had agreed to or signed up for something that sounded good at the time, but now that I was there, I felt like it was a mistake. *Why do I put myself in these incredibly uncomfortable positions?*

My mind was scolding me for signing up for this mastermind when they called my name. I quickly reminded myself that it was natural to be fearful of a new situation. Instead of yelling at myself, I should be patting myself on the back for stepping out of my comfort zone and trying something new to stretch myself. By changing my mindset, I was able to regroup, and I got through the introduction, and it was fine. I basically said I had no idea what I was doing, that I had just become a network marketer with no experience. The comments in the chat after my introduction were warm and welcoming. *What a relief!* John, the leader, stressed the importance of not only regularly attending the meetings, but of making relationships with other group members. He urged us to reach out and schedule one on one sessions with each other.

As others introduced themselves, I made sure to write down those who I would like to get to know better and those I wouldn't. I made it my mission to be proactive and reach out and schedule zoom meetings with each of them. Every one of them was passionate, kind, and honest. With some there was that instant connection where you just knew deep down in your soul that you had just met a lifelong friend. They were all such a giving group of people. Each offered to be there for me with whatever help I needed.

As I listened to each of their stories and saw the reasons behind why they had started their business, I was feeling a bit jealous. Jealous because even though I truly loved the supplements I was selling, it wasn't my passion. I longed to find my purpose just as the others seemed to have found theirs. For my entire life, I had been searching for the answer to this question. *What is my purpose?* I had surmised that some find the answer, while most don't, and I was in the "most" category.

As I listened to my new friends tell me about their coaching business', helping women get through a divorce and to love their bodies, I realized I had decades of experience caring for my loved ones. Maybe that was my purpose. Maybe that's the reason this has been such a big part of my life. I had taken care of my father for thirty years. As a mom, of course, I was a caregiver to both my boys, but Sam's developmental issues took caregiving to a different level. And then more recently, I'd been Gary's caregiver. So much of my life had been filled with constant stress. Looking back, I'm not sure how I had even survived.

Then it dawned on me. I had learned the importance of self-care. This is how I was able to survive. It had taken me thirty years to come to that realization, so maybe I could help other caregivers learn this same lesson sooner. I finally found what I had been searching for. I now knew my purpose was to help other caregivers, and I was all in. With the help of my new friends, I came up with a name for my business—Caregiver Support Squad. There was so much to do to make my dream a reality, but I felt an electricity each day when I woke up. A kind of electricity that I had never experienced before. For the first time in my life, all I wanted to do was work.

I had so much to learn, and I couldn't wait. There weren't enough hours in the day. I even stopped watching TV. In the past, there was never a time where I chose not to watch TV. Honestly, I could never have imagined a world without TV. It was something that relaxed me and took my mind off my problems. Now, I didn't want it, I no longer needed it. The Caregiver Support Squad was all consuming.

Once I had the name, I needed the website. I started to try and build it myself, but quickly realized I needed help. One of my new friends referred me to a friend of hers, Shana, who could help me. At the end of our introductory call, Shana gave me the option of individual coaching, group coaching, or taking one of her virtual courses. I knew I wanted individual coaching, but I was having some serious sticker shock once again. I had not been prepared to spend this kind of money. I didn't have a money tree growing in my yard, and I was still dealing with my IRS issue. However, if I really was serious about this business, I knew I needed Shana. I felt like this was the moment of truth. There was a fork in the road, and I needed to choose which path I'd take. I chose Shana.

She and I would meet weekly via zoom. She took me through a series of exercises to help me clearly define my business. She would give me homework assignments that required a lot of digging deep to come up with the answers. In the meantime, I was still a part of the mastermind group. I continued to make new friends and learn so much from everyone. Some of the group members offered free, weekly get-togethers. Some focused-on mindset and others on business strategies. I attended as many as I could. I was a sponge who longed to soak up as much information as possible.

As for my regular nine to five, the girls I worked with at my agency were incredible. I explained to them what I was doing, and how I planned on spending a small part of the workday, concentrating on the Caregiver Support Squad along with the insurance business, but my insurance clients took precedence over all else. They were all incredibly supportive and impressed by my stepping out of my comfort zone and taking a risk. After a day at the office, I would come home and continue working on my new venture. I was still handling all my other responsibilities, but I now had a purpose that energized me every day.

I joined another mastermind group but didn't find it as life changing as the original. However, I met new people with new ideas. I forged friendships. I was living two lives. I had my regular day to day life with my family and friends and a second online life. None of my family or friends had ever experienced this alternate universe that I had discovered, so it was difficult for them to understand. They all couldn't believe what I was trying to do. I think some might have thought I was out of my mind for investing so much time and money into this new venture. There were times where I questioned myself too. However, all it would take was another zoom meeting with Shana, or one of my new zoom friends, to reinforce the fact that I was doing the right thing.

During my journey, I realized that I didn't want to do one-on-one coaching. It was too emotionally difficult for me since I was in the middle of my own caregiving crisis. With my newly found confidence as a public speaker, I wanted to figure out how to get paid to be a motivational speaker. I worked with my story coach (who had ever heard of such a thing) to figure out what my message was, and how I could deliver it best. While in this phase, I learned that many paid speakers had written books. It legitimized them and gave them credibility to be a published author. I knew that would never be me. I was not a great writer, and it wasn't something I liked to do. So many times, over the past year, I had been told that I needed to write a book, but I would always laugh and say maybe someday—even though I knew someday would never come.

I started to pay attention to all the people in my alternate universe who had or were writing books. They were just regular people, like me. They weren't literary geniuses. My impression was that unless you were eloquent and academic, book writing was not for you. I thought about the books that

I enjoyed and none of them were great literary works of art. I appreciated a book that I could relate to and that was easy for me to read. I didn't like a book where I had to think too much. I basically wanted to read a book where it almost sounded like someone was talking to me. Someone who I could relate to and would like to get to know. If this is what I loved reading, maybe there were others who felt the same way.

Even if there were people out there who might be interested in what I had to say, the idea of writing an entire book seemed impossible. I was also curious about the required number of pages I needed for it to be considered a real book. The idea was overwhelming and daunting. Besides, I wouldn't even know where to begin. I had absolutely no idea how to go about doing this. Shana suggested that I just start writing some stories when the spirit moved me. Stories of my life that others might find interesting or inspirational. I began to relive my life, story by story, in my mind.

Around the same time, I had decided to pivot and no longer target an audience of just caregivers. I wanted to deliver a broader message to a broader audience. I had invested a lot of time and money into bringing the Caregiver Support Squad to life, yet I saw it as a failure and a waste of time. Any work I had done, I had done for free. But Shana and my online friends were always there to pick up the pieces and remind me that this was a journey, that nothing was a waste of time. I had learned a lot about myself, and what I wanted and didn't want. They were right. I changed my mindset and was excited to see where my journey would take me next.

By this time, I had so many podcasts that I followed that I didn't have enough hours in a day to listen to them all. Even so, I took great pleasure in finding new shows to listen to. One day, I turned on a new show just to shake things up a bit. The podcaster was interviewing a woman named Lauren, who had a company that helped first-time writers write their books and get their stories out into the world. This woman sounded so genuine in her message and desire to serve others. She seemed like someone who would be patient and kind with a new author. I was immediately intrigued.

The moment I stopped driving, I found her profile on Instagram and started following her. I looked at her website and saw that she was in the process of forming a twelve-week course for new authors. I couldn't even believe that I was even considering this. As already mentioned, I had a laundry list of reasons why I would never write a book. *Why am I even looking at this website? Maybe this is like quitting smoking.* I was a smoker when I was in my teens and twenties. It was around the time that we were learning just how bad it was for you, but I loved smoking and couldn't imagine quitting. I knew in my gut that someday I would have to, but never really wanted that day to come.

Deep down, I had concluded that I would eventually write a book, but now? I wasn't sure if I was ready for it to be my "someday." I quit smoking when I was twenty-seven years old and never touched a cigarette again. I wasn't planning on quitting, but an illness helped me to see that the time was right. Hearing Lauren speak on that podcast was a message to me that now was the time. However, I couldn't bring myself to hit the "join here" button on my computer screen. For days, the idea rolled around in my head. The angel and devil versions of myself were fighting it out, each arguing for their point of view.

A talk with my therapist sealed the deal. We discussed all my concerns, including the fact that Gary had just been diagnosed with a terminal illness and required me to be home with him most of the time. This certainly didn't seem like the right time to embark on a new project. My therapist told me that I needed to give myself a break. I was concerned about not being able to keep up with the pace of the course because I never knew what Gary would need from me on a day-to-day basis. She reminded me that there would be no grade given at the end of the twelve weeks. If I only did a quarter of the work, that's okay. She thought it would be a great distraction. After our session, I hit the "join now" button.

Once I virtually met Lauren, I knew I had made the right decision, but I was still terrified of meeting the others in the group. I was convinced that they would be better writers who had longed to write a book their entire lives. I was concerned about the embarrassment of sharing my elementary school writing style with them and being judged. But I was relieved to hear that our group would be small and intimate. During our first meeting, my fears were put to rest. Each of us were first time authors who were writing different types of books on a variety of topics. They too were scared. Our little group became a safe space to share my fears, knowing that I would find support, not judgment.

Starting was the most difficult part of the journey. The idea that I should sit down and write for more than ten minutes at a time seemed impossible. After writing 3,500 words, I felt like I was on a roll, however, my computer froze as I was writing, as computers do sometimes. I did what all of us non-technical people do, I turned the computer off, waited for a minute and turned it back on. I went back to my document only to find that 3,000 of my 3,500 words were gone. I clicked on any button I could think of to try and find where my words had gone. Writing those 3,000 words had been painful and the thought of losing them made me sick.

After countless, unsuccessful attempts, I took my computer to a professional. I was confident that they would be able to solve the mystery of my lost words, so I was stunned when they told me they were really gone. *Did this guy have any idea how difficult it had been for me to come up with those 3,000 words? He needs to keep searching.* He explained why there was nowhere else to search, and my computer, and I returned home with only 500 words.

I was angry, frustrated and defeated. Clearly, writing a book was not a good idea. If it was, this would never have happened. When I spoke to Lauren, she shared her own similar story as well as other writers' stories. All of them had lost much more than 3,000 words and had found it within themselves to start over. Maybe those were my practice words, and now I was ready. I couldn't throw my hands up in defeat. Doing such a thing would be incredibly shortsighted and that thought alone made me forge ahead.

I struggled to figure out the best format of the book and the stories I wanted to tell. I struggled to consistently take the time to write every day. I struggled with my sentence structure.

The only thing I didn't struggle with was showing up for our weekly sessions. I showed up every week for twelve weeks. I also attended as many online writing sessions as I could. These were sessions where you would hop on zoom with other writers and be writing simultaneously. It was a form of holding yourself accountable. I had to show up because I had signed up. I learned so many tips and tricks. I learned that everyone struggles to find the right words, not just me.

As I progressed through my stories, I was able to sit and write for much longer stretches of time. I was no longer looking at the clock every few minutes or checking my word count. I began to look forward to my writing time, not all the time, but I still showed up. I realized that I hadn't truly believed in myself. I figured I wouldn't be able to or the fact that my life was out of my control would be the perfect excuse to abandon the mission. Everyone would certainly understand based on my current circumstances with Gary being ill.

I'm not sure at what point I crossed that line of doubt. I understood that sharing my experience could help others, but it was a terrifying concept. It was intimidating to share my intimate thoughts and secrets with anyone because I was fearful of the embarrassment and judgment I might face. However, I now know that pushing through your fears is the only way to grow. It's incredibly hard, but always worth it in the end.

In the last year, I've learned to listen to my gut and trust my judgment. Sometimes, I took a leap of faith, which on the surface looked like it hadn't worked out, but in hindsight it taught me something. I have a cavalry of new friends who are always there to help. It's crazy to think that I've never met any of them in person. What kind of crazy world is this where you work and develop relationships with people who you have never met?

If you told me everything that I've done and tried over the past year, I would never have believed it. It's been a year since I joined the mastermind with my goal of learning how to sell supplements. And I would've bet ten-million dollars that I wouldn't be writing my own book. It seemed ridiculous and outrageous just a year ago. My life changed forever the day I clicked on the zoom link for our first mastermind meeting, when I discovered an alternate universe.

Not a day goes by that I am not forever grateful. This last year has shown me that I do have control of my life and that realization has changed everything. All my dreams are back on the table even at the age of fifty-nine. Nothing feels impossible anymore.

❤ 29 ❤

The End of an Era

"If tears could build a stairway, and memories a lane, I'd walk right up to Heaven and bring you home again."
—Anonymous

Gary had been sleeping in our downstairs office for over a year, so it was nothing new. Due to his various illnesses, he was in a lot of physical pain. He had been suffering for such a long time, but his pain level and anxiety seemed to be heightened soon after he returned home from the psychiatric hospital. On December 16, 2022, he was the happiest I had seen him in months when Ben returned home from college for break. Gary hadn't seen Ben at Thanksgiving because he had been in the hospital. So, it had been four months since they saw each other, and Gary's smile returned for the first few days after Ben returned home.

Gary started becoming extremely anxious sleeping downstairs alone, so I set up an air mattress in our family room, so I could be there for him whenever he needed me. His pain medication was increased, which caused him to be unsteady on his feet at night. He had already fallen a few times in the last few weeks, and I was scared it would happen again, and he would break his hip or a limb.

On Christmas night I heard him coughing a bit. Sam had a cold, so I was concerned that Gary did as well. I asked him about it and he said it was nothing. I never heard him cough again so assumed he was fine. He was tired and didn't feel well overall, which could have been a side effect of the increased pain medication. A couple of nights later, after he told me he was really feeling lousy, I tried to take his blood pressure and temperature. He gave me a hard time and eventually we compromised on only taking his temperature.

It was 102 degrees, which was dangerous for someone in his condition. I told him we needed to go to the hospital, but as always, he refused. He told me he was done with hospitals, and I should just give him Tylenol. Gary had always been extremely stubborn. I don't recall there ever being a time, in our thirty years together, when I was able to convince him to change his mind. I pleaded with him, but it made no difference. He was not going.

The fever and Tylenol dance continued for another thirty-six hours until 6 a.m. on December 29, 2022, when he woke up to use the bathroom and was confused and couldn't walk. It seemed that his legs were almost paralyzed. Somehow, I got behind him, wrapped my arms around his belly, and tried to walk him into the bathroom. We made it in there, but I couldn't get him to turn his body, and he wound up on the floor. I told him I would need to call 911, yet he refused. He didn't want them to come because they would want him to go to the hospital. I ran upstairs, woke up Ben and had him come to help me, but we couldn't get him up. I told him I had no choice but to call.

Once the EMTs arrived, they got him up and in a chair. Once they took his vital signs, they explained that he needed to go to the hospital. He refused. They tried to come up with different arguments that would hopefully persuade him, but nothing worked. As they were walking out the front door, they quietly told me that they would be back later today either because he was unresponsive, or he would change his mind.

They were right. At noon, his temperature was 103 degrees, and his breathing was labored. I told him I was done with this, and he was going. He didn't argue. I'm guessing that he was scared because breathing was beginning to become difficult. As I helped him get dressed (even though I told him it wasn't necessary), he asked why it was taking them so long to get there.

"Really, are you really asking me this now?"

"Really, are you really giving me a hard time now?" he replied, and with that, they arrived.

Gary was scared, and asked if I was coming with him, which seemed like a strange question since there was never a time when I hadn't gone. I told him I would see him in the emergency room, and off they went. I was a bit panicked and misplaced my phone, which delayed my departure by five minutes. I then flew out the door with a bag packed with all the things Gary always asked for in the hospital. Unfortunately, we had become pros at this hospital thing.

I arrived to find a packed waiting room with people coughing and vomiting. I was told to wait until a receptionist could check me in. After ten minutes, I asked if someone would see how he was, and if the doctors needed to speak to me—Gary couldn't answer any questions regarding his medications and disorders. I wanted to make sure the doctors knew his entire history. The receptionist went into the back to check for me. She came back five minutes later, telling me that Gary hadn't arrived yet. *How could that be?* I explained that the ambulance had left at least five minutes before I had.

She told me to wait, once again. As I stood there, panic set in. They checked one more time for me, and I yelled, asking how they could lose a dying man. I ripped my mask off, bolted through the doors, and called 911 to find out where my husband had been taken. At this point, I was crying hysterically. I'm not sure how the man on the other end of the line could understand what I was saying, but he did. Maybe it was part of the training to become a 911 dispatcher.

He explained to me that the ambulance had to meet up with a medical team on the route to the hospital. He couldn't tell me much more, but the ambulance was pulling in as I was on the phone, so I ran to see what had happened. One of the paramedics stopped me before I could see Gary. He explained that he had gone into respiratory failure in the ambulance, and they asked him if he wanted to be intubated, and he agreed. Gary was on a ventilator.

My head was swirling, trying to process what had happened. Gary had not wanted any life saving measures but, at the moment, he had agreed. I thought about how anxious he would be once they were ready to take him off the ventilator. I'd heard from several people that it was such an awful experience. I told myself not to worry about that now. All I wanted to do was see him and speak to a doctor. When I returned to the emergency room lobby, I sat at the admissions desk and answered all the questions about insurance, living will, etc. Once we were done, the woman led me into the emergency room, not to see Gary, but to wait in a private, very comfortable waiting room. She advised me that a doctor would be in to speak with me soon.

The emergency room doctor told me that Gary was critically ill. He was in septic shock, and they were running tests to see the cause of infection. He asked me some questions and explained the next steps. He then took me into the ICU where Gary had been brought. The sight of him was initially quite shocking. He was hooked up to more machines than I had ever seen, and that's saying something since I've had a lot of hospital experience over the years.

I sat in the room for hours while a nurse was monitoring his vitals every minute. Sam called to see how he was doing and asked if he could speak to him. I told him he was resting and unable to talk. I wrestled with how much I should really tell him and Ben. One of Gary's palliative care doctors had been by to see me, and he explained the severity of the situation, yet there was something in his voice that led me to believe Gary would be okay. I did not want to worry Sam and Ben for no reason. I decided to wait and see what the next day would bring.

At 6 a.m. the next morning, the phone rang. It was a doctor explaining to me that Gary's body was shutting down. They had done everything in their power, but it wasn't enough. The doctor told me to get there as soon as possible, so I threw on my clothes and ran out the door while the boys were sleeping. I didn't want them to see Gary hooked up to so many machines, with a tube down his throat. I also knew firsthand that watching someone's body shut down could be very unpleasant. Sam and Ben didn't need to see that.

Once I arrived, the nurse explained how she was going to turn off all the IV medications, and then I would need to leave the room while they removed the respirator. I could then come back in, and she didn't anticipate that Gary would live very long once everything had been shut off. Just a few minutes later, Mindy walked into the room. She didn't want me to be alone. I hadn't wanted to burden her, but I was so glad she was there.

I had my hand on Gary's shoulder while the nurse started to disconnect the IV medications. I turned to say something to Mindy, when the nurse said, "He's gone." He hadn't even lasted long enough to shut everything down. He was done suffering. Finally, no more pain. My Gary was at peace.

And I became a widow on December 30, 2022.

Even though I knew this day would eventually come, I wasn't prepared. *How could this be?* After all, I had known for months that Gary's days were limited. Until you live and experience it for yourself you can't fully understand. After being one half of a team for thirty years, flying solo is tough. I tell myself that Gary was not a functioning partner anyhow, so it shouldn't really feel much different, but it does.

Just a few months earlier, I could ask his opinion on something. If there was a maintenance issue in the house, he could tell me who to call or what to do. Gary was the only person who loved Sam and Ben as much as I did. He was the only one who had been there to watch them grow every day, alongside me. I am now the only parent, and it's overwhelming.

I'm truly blessed to have so many wonderful, caring people in my life, but it's not the same. They keep me busy, but at the end of the day, I come home to a house without Gary and reality kicks in again. The ache and pain leave a hollow feeling in my gut. It's a type of loneliness that makes me feel as if I'm on an island with no other people. Alone with no one beside me.

On second thought... maybe I can!

♥ 30 ♥

Conclusion

"You've always had the power my dear, you just had to learn it for yourself." –Glinda the Good Witch

So, there you have it. I've shared with you many of the highlights from the past fifty-nine years of my life. Why did I feel compelled to be vulnerable and expose myself to you? To illustrate that we all have circumstances that are out of our control. Despite those circumstances, we still have the power to take charge of ourselves and our lives.

To be honest, I almost didn't write this book because I felt my life was ordinary, and my stories wouldn't be impactful or inspirational. Thankfully, I haven't experienced the big T traumas of being sexually abused, kidnapped, or being left alone on a mountaintop. My life has been about little t traumas, which seemed inconsequential when I compared myself to others.

I was suffering from comparison-itis, which is the compulsion to compare yourself to others to determine your relative importance. This is still a tough one for me. I was telling myself that my story would have no impact on people because it didn't compare to others' trials and tribulations. Once I stopped comparing myself to everyone else, I realized that people might be able to relate to my story, because each of us has our own unique set of thoughts and challenges. Even though my stories differ from yours, they are just about the struggles of regular, ordinary day to day life.

I also wasn't going to write this book because I was scared. I feared exposing myself by revealing some of my innermost secrets and thoughts. I was scared that I would be judged for my quality (or lack thereof) of writing, since I don't consider myself to be a writer. I was scared I would be judged for some of the decisions I've made in my life. I was scared I would start writing and never finish. The book would be added to the pile of endeavors I've embarked upon but never completed.

How did I get past all these fears? I reminded myself why I wanted to write this book in the first place. My reason was to help others. I had gone through my life thinking I was a victim of my circumstances. Things happened to me and because of those life events I'd experienced, the path of my life had been predetermined. I was just unlucky. My story had been written for me by other people and circumstances that were out of my control. I figured the only choice I had was to just ride it out, hoping one day to retire and enjoy myself. I had no plan or purpose. I was letting everything and everyone else control my destiny.

I learned from a very early age that I was not worthy because I was overweight. This message was reinforced time and again. I was not thin enough to wear the dance costume. I couldn't buy clothes in regular stores. I couldn't eat certain foods because there was something wrong with me and eating more would only make it worse. I didn't look fit and trim like the rest of my family. I couldn't run fast. I was called every nickname in the book. I was hit with a belt because I was bad. Boys only liked me as a friend. I didn't need any more proof to know that I was unworthy, and it hurt like hell.

I know that most people who shaped my beliefs were not doing it intentionally. My parents were doing what they thought was right. They were doing what they felt would help me. As an adult, I struggled for years thinking that my insecurity and lack of confidence was because of them. I needed someone or something to blame, and who better than your parents? It took me a long time to realize that I was wrong. My parents loved me more than anything and would never do anything to intentionally hurt me. Just like I would never intentionally hurt my children.

I especially struggled with the decisions my mom had made. I blamed her for causing my weight issues by hiding food and putting me on diets at such a young age. I blamed her for not letting me come home from college to be there for my dad. I blamed her for divorcing my father when he became sick, leaving his caregiving in my hands at too young an age. I blamed her for forcing me to move out because of her ex-boyfriend, Dick. I blamed her for being tough on me. I pretty much blamed her for all the crappy circumstances in my life.

What a jerk I was! It's funny how you begin to see things differently once you allow yourself to view circumstances from a different perspective. As an adult and a parent, I now understand how and why she made many of the decisions she did. I now understand that those decisions were not made to intentionally hurt me, but to help me. I now know that it's because of my mother that I have become the person I am today. She set an example for me. She was and still is a strong, smart, tough, independent woman. I'm proud to call her Mom.

My mom is not the cause of my struggles. She was my convenient excuse. She was my excuse not to look in the mirror and take an honest, hard look at who I really was. It was too painful to think that I was the one who hadn't taken ownership. By blaming my mom and others, I was letting myself off the hook. It was everyone else who was the problem and not me.

As a little girl, I lived my life in fear. I feared some of the typical things that children fear like the dark, monsters under my bed and being alone. In addition, I was afraid of being seen because I was convinced, I would be judged. Looking back, I now know that not every person I encountered was judging me, but as a girl, it felt like they were. I know most children (and adults) are bullied at one time or another and some rise to the occasion and others shrivel. I was a prune!

I became a young adult who lacked confidence and self-esteem. All those childhood fears were still with me but when my dad had the stroke, I felt I had no choice but to be there for him. I needed to become his advocate, which required me to learn to speak to doctors, lawyers, and managers. I became a bit more self-assured with each conversation I had, but it was a slow process. If I weren't forced into the situation, I might still be hiding under my bed at the age of fifty-nine.

Life's circumstances pushed me out of my comfort zone repeatedly, and I plowed forward kicking and screaming. After becoming confident in my caregiver role, I stretched and tried personal ads and blind dating thanks to Joe's love and support. Even though the outcome was excruciatingly painful, I had tried and survived. With Gary by my side, it became much easier to move to New Jersey and open my own insurance agency.

Those first years were some of the toughest of my life. I regretted my decision thousands of times in the first eighteen months, but in the end, it was one of the best decisions I had ever made. It allowed Gary and I to have flexibility throughout our lives. I didn't have to answer to anyone when I needed to come in late each morning because I first had to visit my fertility doctor. Gary and I were able to job share and didn't need to hire childcare. Between the two of us, we were full time parents. And when Sam received his diagnosis, I had the flexibility to take him to whatever therapy he needed regardless of time or location.

More recently, when Gary became ill and needed me to care for him 24/7, I was there. I had built a team of women who were caring, conscientious, and committed to both our customers and to Gary and me. Thanks to them, I was able to be there for Gary when he needed me the most, and I'll be forever grateful. If I had remained a CPA, working for someone else, none of these things would have been possible. Imagine how different my life would have been if I had let fear stop me?

Turning fifty caused me to pause and consider the trajectory of the remainder of my life. For the first time I honestly answered the tough questions "when I die, will I have any regrets?" "When I die will I have lived the life I wanted to, as opposed to what was expected of me?" My answers were not what I had hoped, and I realized that I had the power to change those answers. So, I began to chart a course and make one small step at a time.

I began to lose weight once again, but that time was different. Different because I changed my mindset and beliefs. I stopped all the excuses I had been using to justify my issues. It was my mother's fault, I had a slow metabolism, I was big boned, and I was just unlucky. Nonsense! Nonsense! More nonsense! It had been my choice all along and that would be okay if that's what I wanted, but it wasn't. I thought the rest of the world was eating pints of ice cream after each meal and remained thin. Maybe there is a very small percentage of adults who can do that, but I now know most can't.

I had to come to terms with the fact that eating healthy would need to be a lifelong goal, not a diet train I hopped on and off. I had to abolish that "all or nothing" thinking. There would be times when I would slip and not eat healthily, but that didn't give me permission to never eat a carrot again as long as I live. Realizing that I would never be on a diet again was helpful. Instead of being on a diet, I will forever be on an "eat as healthy as I can" plan. Sometimes it works and other times it doesn't. The difference is that now when it doesn't work, I reassess and try something different instead of quitting.

Once I tasted some success with my weight, I was much more comfortable doing uncomfortable things like belly dancing and public speaking. I started to learn to listen to the little voice in my head. The one that wanted to take a chance or try something new. Instead of ignoring her, I leaned in, and it felt darn good.

It's funny how listening to one podcast several years ago led me down a path full of twists, turns, and forks in the road. Each time, I listened more to the little voice in my head. At first, I would get frustrated if a decision I made seemed to be wrong, until I was reminded that there are no wrongs. When something wasn't working, it gave me valuable information. Information and knowledge I could use moving forward.

Listening to that first podcast led to this moment. This moment of you reading my story. If you had told me eighteen months ago that I would be a widow, finishing her memoir, I would have laughed at the absurdity of that statement. It all would have sounded ridiculous and impossible. Obviously, I could not control the quick decline of Gary's health. I would do anything to have that power, but I don't. However, my bold, brave decisions, the things I could control, I have. I trusted myself enough to take not one, but many leaps of faith.

Never in my life have I been more excited to get out of bed each day and get to work. For the first time in my life, I am doing something that feeds my soul. My life's purpose is now to make sure that everyone on the planet understands they alone have the power to control their own destiny.

No more excuses. No more victim mentality. You need to understand you will face adversity because that's life. You might not be able to control your circumstances, but you can always control how you react to them. You can do this! *Anyone* can do this! You just need the desire and the belief. The desire to live your life the way you want to live it, instead of how others think you should. Remember, we only get one shot at this game of life. The power is in your hands.

I've shared some of my favorite quotes within these pages, but I want to leave you with my own, which may have been inspired by one of the last lines Harry utters to Sally at midnight in one of my favorite movies, *When Harry Met Sally*.

"I came here tonight because when you realize you have the power to control your life, you want the rest of your life to start as soon as possible."

Your life starts NOW!

Epilogue

It's now been almost three months since Gary has passed. The life I knew is no longer. I'm now beginning a new chapter. I don't know where it will lead, and there are moments when I question my ability to persevere. Watching my boys grieve is heart wrenching. As a mom I just want to make it all better for them, but I can't. All of us must mourn in our own way and time.

Two weeks after Gary died, I had two big deadlines to meet. The first was to submit my first draft of this book to my editor. Of course, she told me I could extend the deadline and take as long as I needed under the circumstances, but I didn't accept the offer. I needed to focus on something other than the large hole in my heart. It was a challenge to remain focused and, in the process, I often found myself with tears streaming down my face, but I did it. My first draft made it into my editor's hands on the due date.

The second deadline requires me to share some history for context: Back in 1984, when I was in college in Washington, DC, I discovered a store in the old post office pavilion where they only sold items containing hearts. I remember walking through the doors and wanting to never leave. I was enveloped by a sea of red and pink hearts. My eyes didn't know where to look first, and I wished I could grab a sleeping bag and spend the night there. Once I knew this magical store existed, I had the need to visit it often. I would beg my friends to accompany me to the store repeatedly.

Ever since I can remember, I have always loved hearts. There's just something about them that brings me joy and makes me smile every time I see one. Maybe it's because hearts represent love or because I love the colors red and pink, but it doesn't really matter.

Hearts make me happy!

I vowed that one day I would own my own heart store. I wasn't sure if I would purchase the store in Washington, D.C. , or I would open my own, but one way or another it was going to happen. Then life got in the way and my dream was quickly forgotten. Forgotten until November of 2022 when some mindless internet scrolling jogged my memory.

I was shopping for something (I don't even remember what that something was), and I typed in "hearts," then it hit me. My dream that had been lost somewhere in the recesses of my brain, reappeared. I had searched for "heart" items my entire life, and this had never happened. I closed my eyes and recalled the happiness I felt standing in that store surrounded by hearts. I googled to see if the store was still there, but it wasn't. And then it hit me. I no longer need a brick-and-mortar store, instead my heart products could be sold online.

My initial thought was that my dream had just been a silly young woman's fantasy, but then sparks began to go off in my mind. *Why is it a silly fantasy? Just because it's almost forty years later doesn't mean it's too late.* It's never too late to make your dreams a reality, and I knew at that moment I was going to make this happen.

The next morning, I contacted a woman I had met in my first mastermind who sets up online stores. I asked her numerous questions to grasp what I'd be committing to if I decided to proceed. I was most concerned about the monetary and time investment it would take. I didn't have much of either. She assured me that it really wouldn't be a big commitment. There was no question in my mind, I was doing this even though I assumed my family and friends would think I was bonkers!

Everything I needed to do to make my dream a reality brought me joy. I couldn't wipe the smile off my face while working on my new project, despite my current circumstances. It brought me sheer delight!

Coming up with a name was tricky. Sure, I had lots of great ideas, but most website names were already taken. One afternoon, I was eating my favorite food in the whole world, ice cream, when the answer, which should have been obvious to me, hit me. There is something else that brings me as much delight as hearts: rainbow sprinkles!

A Sprinkle of Hearts was born!

The store opened on January 14, 2023, two weeks after Gary died. To meet that deadline, I had a long list of tasks to complete in the weeks before the opening. Of course, I had initially picked the date of January 14th because it was a month before Valentine's Day, however, it would have made no difference if I had to postpone and open on January 31st or even April 1st. The deadline was self-imposed, but I didn't want to wait, especially because this store was bringing unadulterated joy into my life, something I desperately needed.

I certainly felt much lighter after completing my first draft and opening my store. I then needed to focus on two other new projects that were in the wings waiting for me to tackle. The first was learning how to cook. You might recall that I never cooked in my life. It sounds ludicrous, but it's true. I literally never cooked a piece of chicken. I told the boys that we would learn together since they were as clueless as me. I was dreading this and wished a magic genie would descend into my kitchen and prepare all our meals for us. However, I now know that wishing is never the answer, the answer is doing.

My friend Leslie, who is an excellent cook and a very patient teacher, spent an afternoon with Ben and me. She gave us her version of the "introduction to cooking" class. The three of us went to the supermarket, and she pointed out items we could use to make simple, delicious meals. She gave us a lesson on how to pick meat and vegetables. We then returned home, and she showed us how to chop onions and peppers and together we made our dinner.

Leslie gave us permission to fail. Gary was extremely particular about the right way (according to him) to cut, cook, and store food. He couldn't handle watching any of us try to do anything in the kitchen without constantly correcting us. It was stressful so we just never did a thing. Now we had Leslie telling us that the worst thing that could happen was it tasted awful, and we had to throw it out. Even if that happened, we would gain some knowledge and would learn from our mistakes.

I also purchased an air fryer and started experimenting with it. I was stunned at just how good it felt when one of the boys complimented my cooking. It spurred me on and gave me the courage to try new recipes. Did I love it? Nope. However, I don't hate it, and I'm doing it, so that's progress. I was positive that I would never learn to cook in my lifetime. It was a perfect example of why you should "never say never."

"I can't" or "I don't do that" were phrases that until recently were a part of my vocabulary. They would be followed by things like cooking, crafts, or camping. These were all things I just didn't do. Period. Full stop. But now I remind myself of my goal to not give into the "I cant's" and to be brave enough to try. I have set a goal for myself to continually strive to learn new things. In late December, the week before Gary died, I was ready to try something new, and I was discussing my options with my friend Betsy.

Betsy had always enjoyed knitting, which I never understood. I thought only retired, old ladies knit while rocking on their porch in a rocking chair. It seemed time consuming and not worth the time and effort. I appreciated it when I was given a gift that someone created with their own hands, but ordering gifts online worked just fine for me. As Betsy and I were talking, I shared with her that I was reading Michelle Obama's latest book, *The Light We Carry,* and in the beginning, Michelle describes how she began knitting during the pandemic. Her description piqued my interest a bit. She mentioned how it was calming and described it as almost meditative.

So, Betsy asked me, "Do you want to try knitting?" I didn't answer her question directly, instead I started explaining to her why I couldn't do it. She listened to me go on and when I finally paused to take a breath, she asked me, "What about maybe I can? Maybe learning to knit should be your new goal." *She has me*, I thought. I thanked her for reminding me of my aspirations and said I would give it a try.

An hour later Betsy was at my door with knitting needles and yarn. We sat at my kitchen table on December 26, 2022, and Betsy showed me how to knit and purl. She told me I was a natural and complimented me on how quickly I had picked it up. It felt stilted and awkward but something about it was enjoyable. Gary wandered into the kitchen and Betsy asked him if he would like it if I made him a scarf. Gary chuckled because he was doubtful that I would ever do such a thing but smiled and said sure. He would like a pink scarf. He loved pink and orange and was always comfortable with his masculinity.

I practiced for a few days until Betsy said I was ready to start my pink scarf. She was kind enough to go to the store and purchase the materials I needed. This coincidentally happened to be the day that Gary went into the hospital, December 29, 2022. Betsy came to the waiting room in the ICU to give it to me thinking it might keep my mind occupied while I sat with Gary. The whole thing was surreal. It was hard to wrap my head around the fact that my husband was critically ill and there I was knitting him a scarf.

I put my knitting aside for a week after Gary passed away, but when I picked it back up, I found it calmed my mind. I was so focused on the stitches that I wasn't thinking about anything else. I wasn't letting my mind run wild with worry and my massive to-do list. Instead, I listened to an audiobook and knit. When I made a mistake, Betsy would come over and fix it, so I wouldn't need to stop for long and continue to make progress.

I found myself looking forward to it and had to drag myself away when it was time to go to sleep. *I'm a knitter! How the heck did this ever happen?* How much proof did I need to see how I had been shutting myself off to all the possibilities that exist in life? Reflecting on my life, I see how I wasn't really living, but just surviving. I don't know about you, but I want to embrace life by opening myself up to new people and experiences.

I'm still working on removing the phrase "I can't" from my vocabulary. I *know* I will be okay. It's both terrifying and thrilling, but I'm excited to see what lies ahead on this journey. I no longer allow my mind to stop at my initial, negative thinking.

On second thought, maybe I can!

Acknowledgments

To Gar - There's not a single day that goes by where I don't long to talk to you and embrace you once again. Our love may not have resembled the love found in romantic novels, but it was built on a foundation of day-to-day devotion and unwavering commitment to one another. Our playful teasing and occasional quarrels only served to highlight the authenticity of our love, flaws and all (especially yours, LOL). Together, with the assistance of Dr. Roseff, we created the two greatest gifts of our lives—Sam and Ben. My love for you will endure throughout eternity.

To Sam and Ben - Despite your amused eyerolls, I know you always support me. I hope this book inspires you to embrace limitless possibilities and live life to the fullest, fueled by hard work and determination.

To Yogi - Grateful for your unconditional love, you are truly the sweetest and most loving dog on this planet.

To Mom - I am so grateful for everything you have done for me. You have taught me so much about life, love, and everything in between. You have always been there for me, no matter what. You have shown me what it means to be a strong, independent woman. You have taught me to be confident and to stand up for myself. I love you so much.

To Dad - I am grateful for the cherished gift of being Daddy's little girl. I love you and miss you every day.

To Aunt Judy (St. Jude) - I consider myself the luckiest girl in the world to have you supporting me every step of the way. I love you to the moon and back.

To Michael - You went from being my annoying little brother to best friend and a person I can always count on. I love you more than words can say.

To Grandma Ann - For being a woman ahead of her time and showering me with unconditional love.

To Grandma Gerry, Grandpa Hy, and Grandpa Al - Thank you for your love and for believing in my potential even when I couldn't see it myself.

To Joe - You revived joy and laughter in our lives with your love, and I am truly grateful.

To Mindy - Your role in my life extends far beyond that of a cousin. I treasure the extraordinary connection we share, which unites us as sisters, cousins, and best friends simultaneously.

To Pam - Though we are cousins, you have embraced me as a surrogate sister and I'm eternally grateful.

To Mary - Your loyalty, generosity, and giving nature make you a rare gem on this Earth.

To Poppy and Wheezie - I am grateful for the gift of being your family member without blood ties.

To Joannie - Your companionship on this life journey as my partner in crime is truly invaluable.

To Bobby - You were the most wonderful first love a girl could ever experience.

To Leslie - Your unmatched love, support, generosity, and kindness have touched my heart.

To Betsy - Your creativity, caring, and unwavering support make me feel grateful to have you in my corner.

To Lauren Eckhardt - Your patience, sincerity, and vibrant spirit convinced me that you were the perfect person to guide me through this journey of becoming an author. I can't wait to see what's in store for us next.

To Allison Buehner and Julia Schweitzer, my editors - Thank you for enhancing my message in ways I couldn't have foreseen.

To my fellow writers at Burning Soul Collective Community - I'm grateful for our supportive community of mostly first-time authors as we embark on this exciting journey together.

To Shana - Thank you for showing me what is possible in life and changing my world.

To Mary Jo, Helen, Kathy, and Sandra - Your devoted love and support for Gary and me mean more than words can express.

To Sarah J - I am deeply grateful for your unwavering integrity and for helping me make me dream of owning a heart store a reality.

To Keltie, Ryan, and Lenora - Your creative support behind the scenes has made everything possible.

To Tracie - Your pure kindness and love are heartwarming and unforgettable.

To my cousins, nieces, nephews, and their little ones - You brighten my life, and I love you all dearly.

To my beta readers & launch team - Your time, energy, and uplifting feedback are invaluable.

To all the other people who have been there for me along the way-I am so grateful for your support, encouragement and friendship. You have helped me grow as a person and an author. I am so lucky to have you in my life.

For all the little girls who have ever felt like they don't belong, who have doubted themselves, who have ever felt like they're not good enough - this book is for you.

This book is a reminder that you are not alone. You are loved, you are worthy, and you are enough. You are a beautiful, strong, and capable young woman. You have the power to achieve anything you set your mind to.

Never give up on yourself. Never let anyone tell you that you can't do something. Believe in yourself, and never stop dreaming.

This book is dedicated to you.

On second thought... maybe I can!

So Now What?

Well, by reading this book you have now opened up your mind to the possibilities that exist for you. At least, that was my goal. What I don't want is for you to just put this book on the shelf and forget about it. It's now your turn to embark on your own transformational journey.

Use this QR code to access these links.

But where do you even begin?

Get your free resource.
Visit www.DebbieRWeiss.com/InnerPower (don't forget that "R", it stands for Robin) to receive your free resource on how to begin taking steps to unlock your inner power and start living the life of your dreams.

Learn with me.
I'm here to help you. I am on this journey with you and I'm currently (2023) in the process of putting together programs and resources to help both of us. Visit my website at www.DebbieRWeiss.com often to be the first to know about any new resources I've made available.

Listen to the podcast.
Tune into my podcast regularly for inspiration, tips and strategies. https://bit.ly/Maybeican

Spread the word.
Let your friends and family know that there is another way to live. Share the book and website with them so they can get started, too.

Connect with me.
Make sure to stay in touch with me on social media:
Instagram: debbie.r.weiss
LinkedIn: Debbie Weiss
TikTok: @debbierweiss
YouTube: @debbierweiss
Join our free Facebook Community: "Maybe I can" Facebook Community!

Share your thoughts.
Help more people hear the message from "On Second Thought, Maybe I Can…" by leaving a review on Amazon, Good Reads, or your favorite book platform.

See more of my story.
Don't miss the photos that go along with the stories in the book of myself and some of the others mentioned by going to www.DebbieRWeiss.com/photos

Save money.
For some extra added joy, visit: asprinkleofhearts.com
Enter code: ICAN for 10% off your first purchase.

Hear my story in person.
One of my favorite things to do is to share the message from "On Second Thought, Maybe I Can… LIVE with audiences. If you'd like to have your group or corporation inspired by my stories of transformation, consider having me run a workshop or deliver a keynote at your next event. To book a speaking engagement, contact my team at:
www.DebbieRWeiss.com/Speaking

Take one small step towards your new life. You're worth it!

On second thought... maybe I can!

About the Author

With over 50 years of experience dealing with some of life's toughest challenges, Debbie is an expert in chasing your own dreams in spite of your circumstances. She is an entrepreneur running both an insurance agency and her online store, "A Sprinkle of Hearts", host of the "maybe I can" podcast, inspirational speaker, family caregiver and mother.

She has overcome her own limiting beliefs and fears allowing her to begin to live her best life and her life's passion is to help and inspire others to do the same. In her spare time, Debbie loves to laugh, dance, read and stay active.

You can learn more about Debbie at DebbieRWeiss.com.